MEREDITH'S
SECOND
BOOK
OF
BIBLE
LISTS

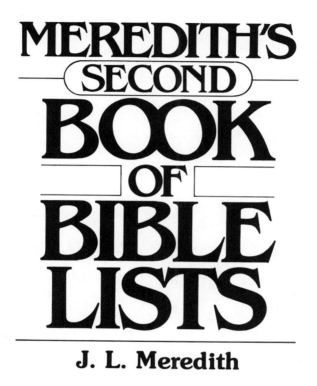

MEREDITH'S SECOND BOOK OF BIBLE LISTS

J. L. Meredith

BETHANY HOUSE PUBLISHERS
MINNEAPOLIS, MINNESOTA 55438
A Division of Bethany Fellowship, Inc.

Published by Bethany House Publishers
A Division of Bethany Fellowship, Inc.
6820 Auto Club Road, Minneapolis, Minnesota 55438

Printed in the United States of America

Library of Congress Cataloging in Publication Data

Meredith, J. L., 1935–
    Meredith's Second book of Bible lists.

    Bibliography: p.
    1. Bible—Handbooks, manuals, etc.   I. Title.
II. Title: Second book of Bible lists.
BS417.M37   1983   220'.0216   83-3807
ISBN 0-87123-319-3 (pbk.)

Dedication

This book is dedicated to my mother, Barbara O'Keeffe.

About the Author

J. L. Meredith's many years of experience in writing technical manuals for the electronics industry has been excellent background from which to draw in preparing the information for his books. His personal, in-depth study of the Bible, his careful research in related materials and his meticulous attention to detail are rounded out by a wry humor—all combining to produce these enjoyable and educational reference works. His first book is entitled *Meredith's Book of Bible Lists.*

Acknowledgments

I wish to pay tribute to the following people for their invaluable help in the preparation and publication of this book.

To my wife, Lorraine, I owe much thanks for her long hours of typing and proofreading. I owe her even more thanks perhaps for her encouragement and her continuous support both as a wife and as a prayer warrior. Her many suggestions for lists were also very helpful.

I want to especially thank the editorial staff at Bethany House for all the work that they have done on this book and on my previous book. They also provided me with many ideas for lists, and they were so kind and patient with me.

I also want to thank the numerous people who wrote to me with suggestions for new lists.

I met a man in Dallas, Texas, who told me that he had given *Meredith's Book of Bible Lists* to his son; it turned his son's life around. That sort of thing makes it all worthwhile!

Table of Contents

150. Eleven Scriptures Commonly Misinterpreted by the
     Jehovah's Witnesses and Mormons

1

Family Affairs

Though the Bible holds a wide variety of themes, the central theme of the Bible is the redemptive role of Jesus Christ. From the fall of Adam and Eve in the garden, God's plan of redemption through the seed of the woman (Gen. 3:15) has been the focal point. It is little wonder that from Genesis 12 onwards, we see the narrowing of God's attention to the family of Abraham and his descendants. From this family Jesus Christ would be born nearly 1900 years later.

Zeroing in on this family necessarily meant zeroing in on the families that came from Abraham. Thus, the Bible is very much a family book, and many of the joys and the frustrations of family life are depicted. Looking over the lists, we find that we have much in common with the families of the Bible: preparations for weddings, the rearing of large families, miraculous pregnancies, twins being born, the devastation of divorce, and death during childbirth. Few of us will have as large a family as some of these people did, however. You'd need a hotel to house them and a farm to feed them.

1. Five Dowries

1. Jacob served Laban for fourteen years so he could marry Rachel (Gen. 29:16-30).
2. "Leah said, God hath endued me with a good dowry; now will my husband dwell with me, because I have born him six sons" (Gen. 30:20).
3. When Shechem the Hivite sought to marry Dinah, her brothers responded, "In this will we consent unto you: If ye will

14

be as we be, that every male of you be circumcised; then we will give our daughters unto you" (Gen. 34:1-16).

4. Boaz obtained Ruth as his wife by purchasing Naomi's property (Ruth 3-4).

5. Saul said, "Thus shall ye say to David, The king desireth not any dowry, but an hundred foreskins of the Philistines, to be avenged of the king's enemies. Wherefore David arose and went, he and his men, and slew of the Philistines two hundred men; and David brought their foreskins, and they gave them in full tale to the king, that he might be the king's son in law" (1 Sam. 18:25, 27).

The wedding at Cana

2. Seven Weddings

1. God gave the bride (Eve) away in mankind's first wedding (Gen. 2:22-24)!
2. Laban made a public wedding feast before deceitfully giving his daughter Leah to Jacob in marriage (Gen. 29:22-25).
3. Samson made a seven-day feast and was given thirty attendants for his wedding. However, the festivities were cut short by Samson's fit of anger, and he never did actually marry the woman (Judges 14:10-20).
4. Jesus told a parable of a king who made a wedding feast for his son. The king invited guests and required that each wear a wedding garment provided for him (Matt. 22:1-14).
5. In another parable, Jesus told of ten virgins who waited at night to accompany the bride and bridegroom to their marriage feast (Matt. 25:1-13).
6. Jesus accepted an invitation to a wedding at Cana. There Jesus performed His first miracle—He changed water into wine for the marriage feast (John 2:1-11).
7. John described the future union of Christ and His Church as a marriage. The Church, Christ's bride, wore fine, white linen (typifying its righteousness). People were invited to the marriage feast (Rev. 19:7-9).

3. Five Divorces

1. Abraham sent away Hagar, who gave birth to Ishmael, at Sarah's urging and God's approval (Gen. 21:9-14).
2. The post-exilic Jews, at Ezra's prompting, divorced their foreign wives (Ezra 10).
3. King Ahasuerus may have divorced Queen Vashti for her disobedience (Esther 1:9-22).
4. God "divorced" the Northern Kingdom for their idolatry (Jer. 3:8).
5. Herod and Herodias both divorced their spouses in order to marry each other (Josephus; cf. Matt. 14:3-4).

4. The Five Men With the Most Wives

1. Solomon had 700 wives and 300 concubines (1 Kings 11:3).
2. King Rehoboam had 18 wives and 60 concubines (2 Chron. 11:21).

3. David likely had over 17 wives, counting his concubines (2 Sam. 3:2-5; 5:13; 20:3).
4. King Abijah had 14 wives (2 Chron. 13:21).
5. Gideon had many wives and 70 sons (Judges 8:30).

5. Ten Miraculous Pregnancies

1. God closed all the wombs of Abimelech's household because Abimelech had taken Sarah for himself. After Sarah was restored to Abraham, Abraham prayed and the women bore children (Gen. 20:17-18).
2. Although Sarah was old, and unable to bear children before, she gave birth to Isaac when she was 90 years old, as the Lord fulfilled His promise. Abraham was 100 years old when Isaac was born (Gen. 21:1-5).
3. After Sarah's death (at which time Abraham was 137 years old), Abraham remarried and fathered more children (Gen. 25:1-6).
4. Rebekah was barren until her husband Isaac prayed for her. Then she conceived and gave birth to twins: Jacob and Esau (Gen. 25:21-26).
5. God opened the womb of barren Rachel, and she gave birth to Joseph and Benjamin (Gen. 30:22-24; 35:18).
6. The angel of the Lord appeared to Manoah's barren wife, foretelling that she would bear a son (Samson) who would begin to deliver Israel from the Philistines (Judges 13:3, 5).
7. The Lord had shut up Hannah's womb, so that she was childless. But then, in answer to Hannah's intense prayer, she gave birth to Samuel (1 Sam. 1:1-20).
8. Although her husband was "too old," the Shunammite woman bore a son, fulfilling Elisha's word (2 Kings 4:13-17).
9. Barren Elisabeth gave birth to John (the Baptist), fulfilling Gabriel's message to her husband, Zacharias. Both Elisabeth and Zacharias were "well stricken in years" (Luke 1:7-9, 13, 18, 57).
10. Jesus was conceived by the Holy Spirit in the Virgin Mary (Matt. 1:18-20; Luke 1:31, 35).

6. Four Sets of Twins

1. The wording in Gen. 4:1-2 suggests that perhaps Cain and Abel were twins.

2. Jacob and Esau (Gen. 25:23-26).
3. Pharez and Zerah (Gen. 38:29-30).
4. The apostle Thomas was called Didymus, which means "a twin" (John 11:16).

7. Women Who Died in Childbirth

1. Rachel died in giving birth to Benjamin (Gen. 35:16-18).
2. Phinehas' wife died right after giving birth to a son. The stress of her delivery was aggravated by her grief at much tragic news—the ark of God was captured, her husband and father-in-law had died, and Israel was defeated in battle by the Philistines (1 Sam. 4:19-22).

8. Youngest Sons

1. Seth was the youngest mentioned son of Adam. Seth's two older brothers were Cain and Abel (Gen. 4).
2. Ham was the youngest of Noah's three sons (Gen. 9:18-24).
3. Jacob was Esau's younger brother (Gen. 25:25, 26).
4. Benjamin was youngest of twelve brothers, all of them sons of Jacob (Gen. 35:16-18; 43:29).
5. Ephraim was the youngest son of Joseph. Ephraim's older brother was Manasseh (Gen. 41:51, 52).
6. Moses was three years younger than his brother Aaron (Ex. 7:7).
7. Kenaz was Caleb's younger brother (Judges 1:13).
8. Jotham was the youngest of the seventy sons of Jerubbaal (Gideon) (Judges 9:5).
9. David was the youngest of eight brothers (1 Sam. 17:12-14).
10. Segub was the youngest son of Hiel. Segub's older brother was Abiram (1 Kings 16:34).
11. Jehoahaz (Ahaziah) was Jehoram's youngest son (2 Chron. 21:16, 17).
12. The prodigal son was the younger of two brothers (Luke 15:11-32).

9. Ten Families with the Most Children

1. Rehoboam had 28 sons and 60 daughters (2 Chron. 11:21).
2. Gideon had 70 sons (Judges 8:30).
3. Ahab had 70 sons (2 Kings 10:1).

The sons of Gideon murdered by Abimelech

4. Ibzan had 30 sons and 30 daughters (Judges 12:8, 9).
5. Abdon had 40 sons and 30 nephews (Judges 12:13, 14).
6. Abijah had 22 sons and 16 daughters (2 Chron. 13:21).
7. Jair had 30 sons (Judges 10:3, 4).
8. Shimei had 16 sons and 6 daughters (1 Chron. 4:27).
9. David had 19 sons and 1 daughter plus an unknown additional number of children by his concubines (1 Chron. 3:1-9).
10. Heman had 14 sons and 3 daughters (1 Chron. 25:5).

Note: It is not known how many children Solomon had.

2

Dwellings

From the Eskimo igloos of the North to the bamboo huts of the Asian tropics, we see a vast array of human dwellings. For some people, a house means barely having a roof over their heads. For others, it means living in a palace of extraordinary beauty and vigilant guards. The contrast in dwelling places are found wherever one goes.

Time has not changed the contrasts in dwelling places. In the Bible we find great men like Elijah and David residing temporarily in caves. We find the glory of the king's palaces in Babylon and the lowliness of tents (such as those of Noah, Abraham, Isaac, and Jacob). Lifeless gods dwelt in temples of grandeur, while powerful men of God, such as John the Baptist, and even the Son of God, had no home of their own.

In this chapter you will learn many interesting facts about Bible dwellings.

10. Eight Important Caves

1. After the destruction of Sodom and Gomorrah, Lot lived in a cave with his two daughters (Gen. 19:30).
2. Joshua trapped five kings of southern Canaan in the cave in which they were hiding. Later they were brought out, killed, and entombed in the same cave (Josh. 10:16-27).
3. The Israelites fled to live in mountain caves and dens to escape the Midianite oppression (Judges 6:2).
4. In Saul's time, Israel again fled to caves and other hiding places to escape the Philistine army (1 Sam. 13:5-7).

5. David used caves as his hideouts and headquarters while Saul sought to kill him (1 Sam. 22:1-2; 23:14, 29).
6. "When Jezebel cut off the prophets of the Lord, . . . Obadiah took an hundred prophets, and hid them by fifty in a cave, and fed them with bread and water" (1 Kings 18:4).
7. When Elijah fled from Jezebel, "he came . . . unto a cave, and lodged there; and, behold, the word of the Lord came to him, and he said unto him, What doest thou here, Elijah?" (1 Kings 19:9).
8. Lazarus was buried in a cave (John 11:38).

11. Five Buildings That Collapsed

1. Gideon "beat down the tower of Penuel, and slew the men of the city" (Judges 8:17).
2. Samson pushed on the two main pillars of a large building and caused it to fall, resulting in the deaths of thousands of Philistines and of Samson himself (Judges 16:23-30).
3. While Job's sons and daughters were feasting in their oldest brother's house, a great wind struck the house, causing it to collapse and kill them (Job 1:18-19).
4. In Jesus' parable, the foolish man's house, built on sand, collapsed when battered by rain, floods, and wind (Matt. 7:26-27).
5. Eighteen people died when the tower of Siloam fell on them (Luke 13:4).

12. Nine Rooftops

1. Rahab the harlot brought the two Israelite spies "up to the roof of the house, and hid them with the stalks of flax, which she had laid in order upon the roof" (Josh. 2:6).
2. "There were upon the roof [of the building that Samson pulled down] about three thousand men and women, that beheld while Samson made sport" (Judges 16:27).
3. Samuel talked with Saul on Samuel's roof (1 Sam. 9:25-26).
4. While walking on his palace roof one evening, David saw Bathsheba bathing, and lusted after her (2 Sam. 11:2-4).
5. "They spread Absalom a tent upon the top of the house; and Absalom went in unto his father's concubines in the sight of all Israel" (2 Sam. 16:22).
6. Some Jews of Ezra's day built booths on their roofs to observe the Feast of Tabernacles (Neh. 8:14-16).

7. Jeremiah prophesied judgment on the houses of Jerusalem because the people were burning incense and offering drink offerings to idols on their roofs (Jer. 19:13).
8. Four men in Capernaum carried a paralytic to the house where Jesus was, seeking his healing. Being otherwise unable to get close to Jesus because of the crowd, they removed a section of the roof and lowered the man on his stretcher to Jesus (Mark 2:3-4).
9. While praying on a housetop, Peter had a vision which led to the first Gentile evangelization (Acts 10:9-16).

13. Fifteen References to Important Tents

1. Jabal "was the father of such as dwell in tents" (Gen. 4:20).
2. Noah lived in a tent (Gen. 9:21).
3. Abraham, Isaac, and Jacob lived in tents as they sojourned in Canaan (Heb. 11:9).
4. Isaac took Rebekah into his mother Sarah's tent on their wedding night (Gen. 24:67).
5. When Jacob finally left Laban, each of the following people had his own tent: Jacob, Laban, Laban's brethren, Leah, Bilhah, Zilpah, and Rachel (Gen. 31:25, 33).
6. The tabernacle in the wilderness was a tent made according to God's specifications. God's presence was there in a special way (Ex. 26:1-4; 2 Sam. 7:6).
7. While the children of Israel were in the wilderness of Sin, they lived in tents (Ex. 33:10).
8. Phineas killed Zimri and Cozbi in Zimri's tent because of their immorality (Num. 25:6-8).
9. Achan took some of the spoils from the battle of Jericho and buried them inside his tent (Josh. 7:21).
10. When Sisera fled from Israel in battle, Jael invited him into her tent to hide. Then, as he slept, Jael drove a tent peg through his temples, killing him (Judges 4:17-21).
11. A Midianite soldier dreamed that a loaf of barley bread had tumbled into the Midianite camp, striking and flattening a tent. His friend interpreted this to mean that God would give Midian over to Gideon (Judges 7:13-14).
12. After killing the giant, David stored Goliath's armor in his own tent (1 Sam. 17:54).
13. After God caused the Syrian army to flee from their camp, four Samaritan lepers, and then all the Samaritans, plundered their tents (2 Kings 7:3-16).

14. David pitched a tent in Jerusalem to house the Ark of God (1 Chron. 15:1).
15. Jonadab commanded his descendants to always live in tents (Jer. 35:6-10).

14. Sixteen Temples

1. About one thousand men and women of Shechem entered the house (temple) of the god Berith for protection from Abimelech. However, Abimelech and his men set fire to the building, killing them all (Judges 9:46-49).
2. During Samuel's earlier years, the Philistines captured the Ark of the Covenant and set it by their idol Dagon in his temple. Twice Dagon fell face down before the Ark (1 Sam. 5:2-4).
3. After Saul was slain, the Philistines "put his armour in the house [temple] of Ashtaroth" (1 Sam. 31:10).
4. Solomon built the temple of the Lord to replace the portable tabernacle-tent (1 Kings 6).
5. Ahab "reared up an altar for Baal in the house [temple] of Baal, which he had built in Samaria" (1 Kings 16:32).
6. When his master worshiped in the house [temple] of Rimnon, Naaman bowed down with him (2 Kings 5:18).
7. Sennacherib was assassinated by his two sons "as he was worshipping in the house [temple] of Nisroch his god" (2 Kings 19:37).
8. The Philistines "fastened [Saul's] head in the temple of Dagon" (1 Chron. 10:10).
9. Nebuchadnezzar carried some of "the vessels of the house of the Lord to Babylon, and put them in his temple at Babylon" (2 Chron. 36:7).
10. After returning from exile in Babylon, the Jews rebuilt the temple, but on a smaller scale than Solomon's temple (Ezra 6:3-15).
11. While in Exile in Babylon, Ezekiel received a very detailed vision of a temple in Israel. He recorded dimensions of pillars, halls, and rooms (Ezek. 40-42).
12. Jesus said, "Destroy this temple, and in three days I will raise it up. Then said the Jews, Forty and six years was this temple in building, and wilt thou rear it up in three days? But he spake of the temple of his body" (John 2:19-21).
13. There was a temple of the goddess Diana at Ephesus (Acts 19:27, 28).

The feast in Belshazzar's palace

14. Believers are called the temple of God, both individually (1 Cor. 6:19) and corporately (2 Cor. 6:16).
15. In John's vision, he was told to measure the temple in Jerusalem (Rev. 11:1-2).

16. "I [John] saw no temple [in the new Jerusalem] therein: for the Lord God Almighty and the Lamb are the temple of it" (Rev. 21:22).

15. Eleven Kings' Palaces

1. "Hiram king of Tyre sent messengers to David, and cedar trees, and carpenters, and masons: and they built David an house" (2 Sam. 5:11).
2. David referred to the temple which Solomon was to build as a "palace ... for the Lord God" (1 Chron. 29:1, 19).
3. It took Solomon thirteen years to build his large, lavish palace (1 Kings 7:1-12).
4. When Zimri's coup failed, he burned Israel's royal palace over himself and died in the flames (1 Kings 16:15-18).
5. Israel's King Ahab coveted Naboth's vineyard because it was close to his palace. When Naboth refused to sell it, Queen Jezebel had him killed (1 Kings 21:1-19).
6. King Pekahiah of Israel was assassinated in his palace in a coup led by Pekah (2 Kings 15:25).
7. When ambassadors from Babylon came to King Hezekiah, the king showed them the wealth in his palace. Then Isaiah prophesied to Hezekiah that his palace would be plundered by Babylon and his sons would serve in the Babylonian palace (2 Kings 20:16-18).
8. Nehemiah served as cupbearer to the king in Persia's royal palace before going to Jerusalem to rebuild the city wall (Neh. 1:1; 2:1).
9. Persia's palace had beds of gold and silver and marble pillars and pavement in the garden court (Esther 1:5-6).
10. King Nebuchadnezzar went insane while walking in his palace (Dan. 4:28-33).
11. The "handwriting on the wall," foretelling the end of the Babylonian empire, appeared on a wall in the Babylonian palace during King Belshazzar's feast (Dan. 5:5).

3

Just for Looks

When was the last time you saw a true hippie—long, greasy hair, tangled moustache and beard, hip-length fringed leather coat, and patched blue jeans? It's been a while. The patched jeans have been replaced by Jordache and Vanderbilt; the leather coat has been succeeded by Izod; the tangled hair has given way to a succession of short, precise styles.

Westerners place great importance upon conforming to the latest styles. Conformity to the style of the day generally guarantees acceptance by others, especially one's peers. Eastern cultures, however, seldom change their styles, but conformity to the style is still important.

Styles may not have been a major issue in Bible times, but any deviation from that style indicated something of real importance. To shave one's head meant one thing, as did pulling out hair. To wear sackcloth was an indication of grief, as was also the use of ashes. One did not tear his garments in public unless he was declaring something. Chains or ropes were another important "apparel" that one might be unfortunate enough to wear.

But to those seeking after God, there is no style or designer label that can match God's custom-designed "garments of righteousness."

16. Haircuts

1. Part of the ceremony for a leper who recovered involved shaving all his hair twice, six days apart (Lev. 14:8-9).
2. The Jews were forbidden to "round the corners of [their] heads," referring to a certain hairstyle (Lev. 19:27).

3. When an Israelite took a Nazarite vow, he was not to cut his hair. When this time of separation was completed, he shaved his head and burned the hair (Num. 6:5, 13, 18).
4. The Levites shaved their whole bodies as part of the ceremony consecrating them to the Lord (Num. 8:5-7).
5. If an Israelite took a woman from among the captives in war to be his wife, she first had to shave her head (Deut. 21:10-12).
6. When Samson's head was shaved, his strength left him (Judges 16:19).

Absalom caught by his hair in the oak tree

7. Absalom cut his hair once a year because it got too heavy (2 Sam. 14:25,26).

8. When Ezra heard that the Jews were intermarrying with the Canaanites and other nationalities, he was so upset that he pulled hair from his head and beard (Ezra 9:1-3).

9. In another occurrence of wrong intermarriage, Nehemiah pulled out the hair of some men of Judah as he charged them not to intermarry (Neh. 13:23-27).

10. After losing his children and wealth, Job shaved his head in his grief (Job 1:20).

11. The people of Jerusalem were told to cut off their hair in response to the Lord's rejection of them (Jer. 7:29).

12. God told Ezekiel to shave his head and beard, and then use the hair to symbolize Israel (Ezek. 5:1-4).

13. Haircuts were prescribed for the priests. They were not to shave their heads or let their hair grow long (Ezek. 44:20).

14. Paul shaved his head at Cenchrea, in connection with a vow (Acts 18:18).

15. Shaving one's head in relation to a vow is also seen in Acts 21:23-26.

17. Rings

1. When Pharaoh promoted Joseph, he put his own ring on Joseph's finger (Gen. 41:42).

2. Some Israelites gave a freewill offering for the tabernacle and its furnishings from their rings and other gold jewelry (Ex. 35:22).

3. King Ahasuerus of Persia gave his signet ring to Haman. The ring was then used to seal copies of an edict ordering the destruction of all Jews (Esther 3:10-13).

4. After Haman was hanged, Ahasuerus gave his royal signet ring to Mordecai. The ring was then used to seal copies of Mordecai's edict, which reversed Haman's decree and allowed the Jews to take vengeance on their enemies (Esther 8:2-13).

5. When Daniel was thrown into the lions' den, they laid a stone upon the mouth of the den, and the king sealed it with his *signet*. This signet may have been a ring (Dan. 6:17).

6. When the father welcomed back his prodigal son, he ordered that a ring be put on the son's finger (Luke 15:22).

18. Perfume and Cosmetics

1. The holy oil used for anointing Israel's priests was perfumed with aromatic spices (Ex. 30:23-33).
2. Jezebel "painted her face" before meeting with Jehu (2 Kings 9:30).
3. Women in King Ahasuerus' harem were "purified" with perfumes (Esther 2:12).
4. The adulteress of Proverbs 7 perfumed her bed with myrrh, aloes, and cinnamon (7:17).
5. "Ointment and perfume rejoice the heart" (Prov. 27:9).
6. The lovers of the Song of Solomon lavishly used valuable perfumes:
   a. Solomon used myrrh, frankincense, and other spices (1:3; 3:6; 4:6).
   b. His wife used spikenard, camphire, saffron, calamus, cinnamon, frankincense, myrrh and aloes, among others (1:12; 4:10-14; 5:1,5).
7. Jer. 4:30 and Ezek. 23:40 mention fictitious women painting their eyes.
8. Daniel used no anointing oils during his three weeks of mourning (Dan. 10:3).
9. Frankincense and myrrh were given to Jesus by the wise men (Matt. 2:11).
10. A sinful woman anointed Jesus' feet with ointment (perfume) (Luke 7:37-38).
11. Mary (Lazarus' sister) anointed Jesus' feet with expensive spikenard. The odor of the ointment filled the house (John 12:3).
12. On yet another occasion, a woman came to Jesus and poured "very precious ointment" on his head (Matt. 26:7).

19. Chains, Ropes, and Threads

1. When Tamar gave birth, one of her twins "put out his hand: and the midwife took and bound upon his hand a scarlet thread, saying, This came out first" (Gen. 38:28).
2. Pharaoh "put a gold chain about [Joseph's] neck" (Gen. 41:42).
3. Aaron's ephod included gold chains of wreathen work (Ex. 28:14).
4. Rahab dropped a scarlet cord from her window to aid the

spies to leave the city and then she used it later to show them where she lived (Josh. 2:15-19).

5. Gideon claimed for himself the gold chains that were about the necks of the Midianites' camels (Judges 8:26).

6. The Philistines bound Samson with seven fresh cords, but he broke them as soon as the Philistines came to get him (Judges 16:6-9).

7. Samson said, "If they bind me fast with new ropes that never were occupied, then shall I be weak, and be as another man . . . and he brake them from off his arms like a thread" (Judges 16:11-12).

8. Ben-hadad's servants put sackcloth on their loins and ropes on their heads to beg for mercy from King Ahab (1 Kings 20:31).

9. Solomon made chains strung with pomegranates to decorate the temple (2 Chron. 3:16).

10. Nebuchadrezzar "put out Zedekiah's eyes, and bound him with chains, to carry him to Babylon" (Jer. 39:7).

11. Jeremiah was "bound in chains among all that were carried away captive of Jerusalem and Judah" (Jer. 40:1).

12. Belshazzar "clothed Daniel with scarlet, and put a chain of gold about his neck" (Dan. 5:29).

13. The Gadarene demoniac had been bound, but "the chains had been plucked asunder by him, and the fetters broken in pieces" (Mark 5:3,4).

Samson after his capture

14. When the angel woke Peter up in prison, Peter's chains fell off and he was set free (Acts 12:6,7).
15. "The chief captain came near, and took [Paul], and commanded him to be bound with two chains; and demanded who he was and what he had done" (Acts 21:33).
16. The soldiers on Paul's ship cut the ropes holding the lifeboat so that the crew could not escape (Acts 27:30-32).
17. When Paul arrived in Rome, he was bound with a chain (Acts 28:20).
18. John "saw an angel come down from heaven, having the key of the bottomless pit and a great chain in his hand. And he laid hold on the dragon, that old serpent, which is the Devil, and Satan, and bound him a thousand years" (Rev. 20:1,2).

20. Fourteen Colors in the Bible

1. In middle of the fiery cloud in Ezekiel's vision was "as the colour of *amber*" (Ezek. 1:4).
2. "In the fourth chariot [were] grisled and *bay* horses" (Zech. 6:3).
3. "His locks are bushy, and *black* as a raven" (Song of Sol. 5:11).
4. When the Israelite camp moved, various utensils in the tabernacle would be covered with *blue* cloths before being carried (Num. 4:5-12).
5. The "man" that came to Daniel in Daniel 10 had arms and feet "like in colour to polished *brass*" (10:6).
6. "And he [Jacob] removed . . . all the *brown* among the sheep" (Gen. 30:35).
7. "What be these two olive branches which through the two *golden* pipes empty the *golden* oil out of themselves?" (Zech. 4:12).
8. "Then shall ye bring down my *gray* hairs with sorrow to the grave" (Gen. 42:38).
9. "He maketh me to lie down in *green* pastures" (Ps. 23:2).
10. "They put on [Jesus] a *purple* robe" (John 19:2).
11. "It will be fair weather: for the sky is *red*" (Matt. 16:2).
12. "I saw a woman sit upon a *scarlet* coloured beast" (Rev. 17:3).
13. "And I saw a great *white* throne" (Rev. 20:11).
14. "She saw . . . the images of the Chaldeans portrayed with *vermilion*" (Ezek. 23:14).

21. Seven Types of Fabrics

1. "John had his raiment of *camel's hair*" (Matt. 3:4).
2. "And thou shalt make curtains of *goat's hair* to be a covering upon the tabernacle" (Ex. 26:7).
3. "He wrapped [the body of Jesus] in a clean *linen* cloth" (Matt. 27:59).
4. Lydia was "a seller of *purple*" (Acts 16:14).
5. "The sun became black as *sackcloth of hair*" (Rev. 6:12).
6. *Silk* was one of the items which the merchants of the earth sold to Babylon (Rev. 18:11-12).
7. "Your sins . . . shall be as *wool*" (Isa. 1:18).

22. Sackcloth

1. Jacob put on sackcloth when he heard that Joseph had perished (Gen. 37:34).
2. Ben-hadad's servants wore sackcloth before Ahab (1 Kings 20:31,32).
3. Job wore sackcloth (Job 16:15).
4. Jeremiah prophesied that the people of Zion should put on sackcloth in view of the coming destroyer (Jer. 4:8).
5. The elders of the daughters of Zion wore sackcloth (Lam. 2:10).
6. Daniel sought the Lord in sackcloth (Dan. 9:3).
7. Prophecy was given in order that a nation might lament in sackcloth (Joel 1:8).
8. A pagan city wore sackcloth in repentance before the Lord (Jonah 3:8).

23. Uses of Ashes

1. Used as a symbol of mourning (2 Sam. 13:19; Esther 4:1,3).
2. Used as a symbol of repenting (Job 42:6; Dan. 9:3; Jonah 3:6; Matt. 11:21; Luke 10:13).
3. Used as a means of a disguise (1 Kings 20:38,41).
4. Used to sit in (Job 2:8; Isa. 58:5; Jer. 6:26).

24. Twenty-one Instances of Rending of Garments

1. Both Reuben and Jacob rent their clothes when they heard that Joseph had been killed (Gen. 37:29,34).

2. Joseph's brothers rent their clothes upon finding the silver cup in Benjamin's sack (Gen. 44:13).

3. Joshua and Caleb rent their clothes when the people murmured against the Lord about going into the Promised Land (Num. 14:6).

4. Jephthah rent his clothes when his hasty words came back to torment him (Judges 11:35).

5. David and all the men with him rent their clothes when they heard that King Saul was dead (2 Sam. 1:11).

6. David commanded Joab and the people with him to rend their clothes upon the death of Abner (2 Sam. 3:31).

7. Tamar rent her clothing after being raped by Amnon (2 Sam. 13:19).

8. David rent his clothes when he heard that Absalom had taken his revenge upon Amnon (2 Sam. 13:31).

9. Hushai the Archite came to meet David with rent clothes (2 Sam. 15:32).

10. Elisha rent his clothes when Elijah was taken up to heaven (2 Kings 2:12).

11. The king of Israel rent his clothes when Naaman came to him to be healed of leprosy (2 Kings 5:7).

12. The king of Israel rent his clothes when he heard a woman quarreling about eating another woman's son (2 Kings 5:7).

13. Athaliah rent her clothes when Jehoiada the priest put her out of power (2 Kings 11:14).

14. King Hezekiah rent his clothes when Rabshakeh denounced the Lord before the people of Israel (2 Kings 19:1).

15. Josiah rent his clothes when the book of the law was read in his presence for the first time (2 Kings 22:11, 19).

16. Ezra rent his clothing when he heard about the mixture of marriages between God's people and the nations around them (Ezra 9:3,5).

17. Job rent his clothes when he heard the evil report (Job 1:20).

18. Job's three friends rent their clothes when they saw Job (Job 2:12).

19. Eighty men came to the house of the Lord with rent clothes (Jer. 41:5).

20. The high priest rent his clothes when Jesus spoke of His being seated at the right hand of God's power (Matt. 26:65).

21. Barnabas and Paul rent their clothes when those who witnessed the miracle at Lystra began to worship them as gods (Acts 14:14).

4

Eat and Drink

There was a time when sitting down for a meal was both enjoyable and relaxing. It was a time to enjoy the family being together and to discuss the expectations and the experiences of the day. People weren't in such a hurry that they had to gulp their meals down. Neither were they so concerned about whether the food was absolutely the most nutritious. Somehow, we have lost some of the benefit of God's purpose for eating and drinking—fellowship and enjoyment.

Eating and drinking form a central role in the activities of people in the Bible. The following sixteen lists show many aspects of this role in their lives. Menus may have changed since then, but the vital role it had in life has not changed. Do these sound familiar: family meals, banquets, meals with friends, marriage feasts, community picnics, discussions about wine and its purposes, times of fasting, times of severe shortage, breads, water, soups, "miraculous" meals you didn't know were coming, strange foods, poisonous foods, and horrible foods? Most of them are familiar to us.

25. Twenty-seven Important Meals

1. The original sin occurred when Adam and Eve ate the fruit of the forbidden tree (Gen. 3:6).
2. When the Lord and two angels came to Abraham in human form, Abraham served a meal to them (Gen. 18:1-8).
3. After leaving Abraham, the two angels went to Sodom. Lot welcomed them into his house and made them a feast (Gen. 19:1-3).

4. Esau sold his birthright for a meal of bread and pottage of lentils (Gen. 25:29-34).
5. Jacob obtained his father's blessing by bringing him a meal and pretending he was Esau (Gen. 27:1-29).
6. When Joseph's brothers went down to Egypt the second time, Joseph (still hiding his identity) invited them to eat with him (Gen. 43:16-34).
7. In the first Passover observance, each Jewish household killed a lamb, applied its blood to the doorposts, roasted the meat, and ate it. God commanded that the Passover meal, plus seven days of eating unleavened bread, be observed annually from then on, in remembrance of Israel's deliverance from Egypt (Ex. 12:1-20).
8. When David's daughter Tamar served some food to her half brother Amnon (who was pretending to be sick), he raped her (2 Sam. 13:1-14).
9. Ravens brought Elijah bread and meat while he hid by the brook Cherith (1 Kings 17:3-6).
10. Later, a widow of Zarephath fed Elijah. Her supply of meal and oil was miraculously replenished during the famine (1 Kings 17:8-16).
11. When Elijah called Elisha to be a prophet, Elisha killed and boiled his yoke of oxen and gave a feast before following Elijah (1 Kings 19:19-21).
12. Queen Vashti was deposed during a seven-day banquet King Ahasuerus gave for people of Shushan (Esther 1:5-21).
13. At the second of two banquets which Queen Esther gave for the king and Haman, she revealed Haman's plot to have all the Jews killed. As a result, Haman was hanged and the Jews were saved (Esther 7).
14. The Jews feasted to celebrate their victory over Haman and their other enemies. Mordecai and Esther made this feast (called Purim) an annual event (Esther 9:17-32).
15. As Job's sons and daughters were feasting in their eldest brother's house, the house collapsed, killing them all (Job 1:18-19).
16. Daniel and his friends chose to eat vegetables rather than defile themselves with the king's food (Dan. 1:5-16).
17. As Belshazzar gave a great feast in his palace, the "handwriting on the wall" announced the end of his kingdom (Dan. 5).
18. The Pharisees criticized the disciples for plucking grain on the Sabbath (Matt. 12:1-8).

19. John the Baptist was beheaded at Herodias' daughter's request after she danced at Herod's birthday supper (Mark 6:21-28).
20. Jesus miraculously fed five thousand men with five loaves and two fish (John 6:5-14). Later He fed four thousand in similar fashion (Matt. 15:32-38).
21. Martha and Mary invited Jesus to their home for a meal. Martha occupied herself with preparation for the meal, but Mary sat at Jesus' feet (Luke 10:38-42).
22. Jesus told a parable of a man who made a great banquet and invited many people. They all turned him down, so he had others brought in from the streets so that his house would be filled (Luke 14:16-24).
23. The father made a joyful feast when his prodigal son returned home (Luke 15:20-25).
24. Mary anointed Jesus' feet with precious ointment while He was their supper guest (John 12:1-3). Jesus was also anointed by women at two other mealtimes during His lifetime (Luke 7:36-50; Matt. 26:6-13).
25. Jesus' "Last Supper" was the Passover meal that He ate with the twelve disciples in the Upper Room (Matt. 26:1-30).
26. Jesus ate three meals with His disciples after His resurrection: He broke bread in Emmaus (Luke 24:30), ate fish at Jerusalem to prove that He was not a ghost (Luke 24:38-43), and ate fish and bread by the Sea of Galilee (John 21:12-14).
27. John witnessed the marriage feast of the Lamb in heaven (Rev. 19:9).

26. Three Forty-Day Fasts

1. Moses neither ate nor drank while he talked with God for forty days on Mount Sinai (Ex. 34:27, 28).
2. The angel of the Lord fed Elijah two meals which gave him strength for the next forty days (1 Kings 19:5-8).
3. Jesus fasted for forty days in the wilderness after His baptism (Matt. 4:1,2).

27. Twenty-four Shorter Fasts

1. The Israelites fasted for the rest of the day after the Benjamites had defeated them in two successive battles (Judges 20:26).

2. The children of Israel repented of their idolatry and fasted with Samuel at Mizpah for a day (1 Sam. 7:3-6).

3. Saul ordered a fast for his soldiers while pursuing the Philistines. His son Jonathan had not heard about it, so he ate some wild honey that day (1 Sam. 14:24-27).

4. When Saul was unsuccessfully inquiring of the Lord, he fasted all day and night (1 Sam. 28:20).

5. The inhabitants of Jabesh-gilead fasted for seven days (1 Sam. 31:11-13) and David and his men fasted the rest of the day when they heard about the deaths of Saul and his sons (2 Sam. 1:11,12).

6. "The Lord struck the child that Uriah's wife bore unto David and it was very sick. David therefore besought God for the child; and David fasted" (2 Sam. 12:15,16).

7. Because her husband Ahab wanted Naboth's vineyard, Queen Jezebel proclaimed a day of fasting as part of a scheme to get it (1 Kings 21:8-10).

8. King Ahab humbled himself and fasted when Elijah accused him of Naboth's murder (1 Kings 21:27).

9. King Jehoshaphat sought the Lord and proclaimed a fast in Judah when the Moabites attacked (2 Chron. 20:1-4).

10. Before leaving Babylonia for Jerusalem, Ezra and his troop sought the Lord and fasted (Ezra 8:21-23).

11. Nehemiah fasted when asking the Lord for favor before the king of Persia (Neh. 1:1-4).

12. The inhabitants of Jerusalem separated themselves from the people of the land and fasted (Neh. 9:1-3).

13. Mordecai and the rest of the Jews in Media-Persia fasted after the king declared that they were all to be killed (Esther 4:1-3,15,16).

14. The people of Judah came to Jerusalem for a fast, and Baruch read them the prophecy of Jeremiah (Jer. 36:9,10).

15. After Daniel had been thrown into the lions' den, King Darius spent the night fasting (Dan. 6:18).

16. Daniel fasted as he sought the Lord for the liberation of his people from Media-Persia (Dan. 9:3,4).

17. Jonah's warning of God's wrath drove the people of Nineveh to repentance, and the king declared a fast until God's wrath was turned away (Jonah 3:4-10).

18. Jesus told the disciples that they should have prayed and fasted in order to gain power over a demon that they had not been able to cast out (Matt. 17:21).

19. Saul fasted for three days in Damascus while he waited for Ananias (Acts 9:9).
20. Cornelius was fasting and praying when an angel appeared to him and told him to send for Peter (Acts 10:1-3).
21. The elders at Antioch fasted and prayed and laid hands on Paul and Barnabas before sending them out as missionaries (Acts 13:1-3).
22. Paul and Barnabas fasted and prayed as they chose elders for each new church (Acts 14:23).
23. Forty men bound themselves by oath neither to eat nor drink until they had killed Paul (Acts 23:20,21).
24. The 275 passengers on the storm-tossed ship with Paul had fasted for fourteen days (Acts 27:33).

28. Winepresses

1. Gideon threshed wheat by the winepress to hide it from the Midianites (Judges 6:11).
2. Gideon's army slew Zeeb the Midianite at the winepress of Zeeb (Judges 7:25).
3. Isaiah spoke of Judah as a vineyard and of God putting them into His winepress of wrath (Isa. 5:1,2; 63:1-4).
4. Jesus told a parable about a householder who planted a vineyard, dug a winepress, and rented it out to tenants (Matt. 21:33-41).

29. Jesus and Wine

1. Jesus turned the water into wine at the wedding in Cana (John 2:1-10).
2. "No man putteth new wine into old [wineskins]; else the new wine will burst the [wineskins], and be spilled, and the [wineskins] shall perish. But new wine must be put into new [wineskins]; and both are preserved" (Luke 5:37,38).
3. "The Son of man came eating and drinking, and they say, Behold a man gluttonous, and a winebibber, a friend of publicans and sinners" (Matt. 11:19; Luke 7:34).
4. "No man also having drunk old wine straightway desireth new: for he saith, The old is better" (Luke 5:39).
5. "And he took the cup, and gave thanks, and gave it to them, saying, Drink ye all of it; for this is my blood of the new testament, which is shed for many for the remission of sins.

An ancient winepress

But I say unto you, I will not drink henceforth of this fruit of the vine, until that day when I drink it new with you in my Father's kingdom" (Matt. 26:27-29).

6. "And they gave him to drink wine mingled with myrrh: but he received it not" (Mark 15:23).

30. Nine Old Testament Admonitions About Wine

1. "The Lord spoke unto Aaron, saying, Do not drink wine nor strong drink, thou, nor thy sons with thee, when ye go into the tabernacle of the congregation, lest ye die" (Lev. 10:8,9).

2. "When either man or woman shall separate themselves to vow a vow of a Nazarite, to separate themselves unto the Lord: he shall separate himself from wine and strong drink, and shall drink no vinegar of wine, or vinegar of strong

drink, neither shall he drink any liquor of grapes, nor eat moist grapes, or dried" (Num. 6:2,3).

3. "It is not for kings, O Lemuel, it is not for kings to drink wine; nor for princes strong drink: lest they drink, and forget the law, and pervert the judgment of any of the afflicted" (Prov. 31:4,5).
4. "Wine is a mocker, strong drink is raging: and whosoever is deceived thereby is not wise" (Prov. 20:1).
5. "He that loveth wine and oil shall not be rich" (Prov. 21:17).
6. "Who hath woe? who hath sorrow? who hath contentions? who hath babbling? who hath wounds without cause? who hath redness of eyes? They that tarry long at the wine; they that go to seek mixed wine" (Prov. 23:29,30).
7. "Look not thou upon wine when it is red, when it giveth his colour in the cup, when it moveth itself aright. At the last it biteth like a serpent, and stingeth like an adder" (Prov. 23:31,32).
8. "Give strong drink unto him that is ready to perish, and wine unto those that be of heavy hearts. Let him drink, and forget his poverty, and remember his misery no more" (Prov. 31:6,7).
9. "Woe unto them that rise up early in the morning, that they may follow strong drink; that continue until night, till wine inflame them!" (Isa. 5:11).

31. Four New Testament Admonitions About Wine

1. "It is good neither to eat flesh, nor to drink wine, nor any thing whereby thy brother stumbleth, or is offended, or is made weak" (Rom. 14:21).
2. "Be not drunk with wine, wherein is excess; but be filled with the Spirit" (Eph. 5:18).
3. Paul wrote to Timothy, "Drink no longer water, but use a little wine for thy stomach's sake and thine often infirmities" (1 Tim. 5:23).
4. "A bishop must be blameless . . . not given to wine" (1 Tim. 3:2,3; Titus 1:7).

32. Fourteen Famines

1. "There was a famine in the land: and Abram went down into Egypt to sojourn there; for the famine was grievous in the land" (Gen. 12:10).

2. "There was a famine in the land, beside the first famine that was in the days of Abraham. And Isaac went unto Abimelech king of the Philistines unto Gerar" (Gen. 26:1).

3. Pharaoh made Joseph the food-storage supervisor in preparation for the impending famine which eventually covered all the earth (Gen. 41).

4. God sent a dense swarm of locusts to destroy all the plants that remained in Egypt after the plague of hail had destroyed most of the crops (Ex. 10:14,15).

5. The Midianites would swoop through the land of Israel during Gideon's time, plundering and destroying all the crops and livestock they found (Judges 6:3-6).

6. Elimelech and his wife Naomi moved to Moab to escape the famine in Bethlehem (Ruth 1:1,2).

7. "There was a famine in the days of David three years . . . because [Saul] slew the Gibeonites (2 Sam. 21:1).

8. Elijah prophesied a draught and Samaria suffered three years of famine until he told King Ahab that it would rain again (1 Kings 17:1; 18:2,41-45).

9. God sent a seven-year famine upon Israel during Elisha's ministry (2 Kings 8:1,2).

10. "Nebuchadnezzar king of Babylon came, he, and all his host, against Jerusalem, and pitched against it; and they built forts against it round about. And . . . the famine prevailed in the city and there was no bread for the people of the land" (2 Kings 25:1-3).

11. The Chaldeans laid siege against Jerusalem, and God allowed famine and pestilence upon the people to judge them (Jer. 32:24,36; 52:6).

12. The penniless prodigal son found himself in the midst of a great famine (Luke 15:14).

13. "And there stood up one of them named Agabus, and signified by the Spirit that there should be great dearth throughout all the world; which came to pass in the days of Claudius Caesar" (Acts 11:28).

14. The rider of the pale horse spreads famine and pestilence over the earth (Rev. 6:8).

33. Seven Miraculous Meals

1. God fed Israel with heaven-sent manna in the wilderness (Ex. 16:11-15).

2. "Ravens brought [Elijah] bread and flesh in the morning, and bread and flesh in the evening" (1 Kings 17:6).
3. The widow of Zarephath made Elijah a cake of bread and, as promised, her cruse of oil never ran dry, nor did her barrel of meal go empty (1 Kings 17:12-16).
4. An angel prepared a meal for Elijah that gave him strength for forty days and nights (1 Kings 19:5-8).
5. Elisha fed one hundred men with twenty barley biscuits. They all ate and still had leftovers (2 Kings 4:42-44).
6. Jesus fed about five thousand men (not including the women and children with them) with only five small loaves of bread and two fish. Everyone ate enough, and leftovers filled twelve baskets (Matt. 14:15-21).
7. Jesus also fed four thousand men (plus the women and children with them) with seven loaves and a few small fish. There were seven basketfuls of food left over (Matt. 15:32-38).

34. Three Soups

1. Jacob traded bread and pottage of lentils for Esau's birthright (Gen. 25:29-34).
2. Gideon fixed a meal for an angel. The meal included a pot of broth (Judges 6:19).
3. Elijah fed the sons of the prophets with a pot of pottage (2 Kings 4:38).

35. Loaves of Bread

1. Twelve loaves of bread were to be left upon the table of shewbread in the tabernacle (Lev. 24:5-7).
2. Three men confirmed Samuel's words to Saul by giving him two loaves of bread as had been prophesied (1 Sam. 10:3,4).
3. David and his men took the twelve loaves of the Bread of the Presence from the tabernacle while Saul was chasing David to kill him (1 Sam. 21:1-6).
4. The widow of Zarephath prepared a loaf of bread for Elijah out of her last bit of meal (1 Kings 17:11-16).
5. Jesus took 5 loaves and fed 5,000 men (Matt. 14:15-21) and later took 7 loaves and fed 4,000 (Matt. 15:32-38).
6. "Jesus took the bread, and blessed it, and brake it, and gave

it to his disciples, and said, Take, eat: this is my body" (Matt. 26:26).

7. The men at Emmaus did not recognize Jesus until He took the bread, blessed it, and broke it (Luke 24:30,31).
8. The Gibeonites fooled Joshua by showing him moldy loaves of bread and telling him that the loaves had been freshly baked for their journey (Josh. 9:12).

36. Sweet and Sour: Flavors in the Bible

1. God commanded Israel to keep the Passover meal by eating a lamb with unleavened bread and bitter herbs (Ex. 12:8).
2. Moses was to make a special anointing oil with olive oil and cinnamon (Ex. 30:23-25).
3. Garlic, onions, and leeks were some of the pleasures of Egypt for which the Israelites longed (Num. 11:5).
4. The Psalmist said, "My meditation of him shall be sweet: I will be glad in the Lord" (Ps. 104:34).
5. "Stolen waters are sweet, and bread eaten in secret is pleasant" (Prov. 9:17).
6. "Bread of deceit is sweet to a man; but afterwards his mouth shall be filled with gravel" (Prov. 20:17).
7. "My son, eat thou honey, because it is good; and the honeycomb, which is sweet to thy taste" (Prov. 24:13).
8. "The full soul loatheth an honeycomb; but to the hungry soul every bitter thing is sweet" (Prov. 27:7).
9. God asks the people why they bother making sacrifices when "your burnt offerings are not acceptable, nor your sacrifices sweet unto me" (Jer. 6:20).
10. "The fathers have eaten a sour grape, and the children's teeth are set on edge" (Jer. 31:29).
11. "Behold, the days come, saith the Lord, that the plowman shall overtake the reaper, and the treader of grapes him that soweth seed; and the mountains shall drop sweet wine, and all the hills shall melt" (Amos 9:13).
12. "Does a fountain send forth at the same place sweet water and bitter?" (James 3:11).
13. Ezekiel ate a book and declared that it was as sweet as honey in his mouth (Ezek. 2:9-3:3).
14. John also ate a book but wrote, "It was in my mouth sweet as honey; and as soon as I had eaten it, my belly was bitter" (Rev. 10:9,10).

37. Five Poisons

1. "The Lord sent fiery serpents among the people, and they bit the people; and much people of Israel died" (Num. 21:6).
2. Elisha "healed" a poisonous spring of water (2 Kings 2:19-22).
3. The sons of the prophets made pottage but accidentally threw in some poisonous gourds. Elisha made it fit to eat again (2 Kings 4:41).
4. James said that the tongue is "an unruly evil, full of deadly poison" (James 3:8).
5. Christ promised, "These things shall follow them that believe; . . . if they drink any deadly thing, it shall not hurt them" (Mark 16:17,18).

38. Instances of Cannibalism

1. A woman in Samaria boiled her son and ate him with her neighbor and then cried to the king when her neighbor would not boil her son (2 Kings 6:24-29).
2. Women boiled and ate their children during the Babylonian siege on Jerusalem (Lam. 4:10).

39. Strange Foods

1. Moses took the *golden calf* "which they had made, and burnt it in the fire, and ground it to powder, and strawed it upon the water, and made the children of Israel drink of it" (Ex. 32:20).
2. God sent *manna* for the children of Israel to eat while they wandered in the wilderness. "Manna" means "what is it?" (Ex. 16:15).
3. Samson ate *honey* from out of a dead lion (Judges 14:8,9).
4. John the Baptist ate *locusts* and *wild honey* (Matt. 3:4).

40. The Biggest Meals in the Bible

1. The Lord fed the entire nation of Israel for forty years on manna (Deut. 8:16).
2. The people complained about the manna, so God sent then quail for an entire month (Num. 11:19,31).
3. "Solomon's provision for one day was thirty measures of

Jesus feeds the 5,000

fine flour, and threescore measures of meal, ten fat oxen, and twenty oxen out of the pasture, and an hundred sheep, besides harts, and roebucks, and fallowdeer, and fatted fowl" (1 Kings 4:22,23).

4. Jesus fed 5,000 men with 5 loaves and 2 fishes and 4,000 men with 7 loaves and a few fish (Matt. 14:19-21; 15:32-38).

5

Water

Rarely does a week go by but that the evening news reports about another city whose wells have been discovered to be contaminated. Life for those depending upon this water sometimes becomes chaotic and frustrating. Though we usually take it for granted, good water is absolutely essential for our survival.

In Bible times water was not taken for granted. The task of drawing water was a daily chore for each family. The following seven lists show this vital role of water in the lives of Bible people. We see the importance of the local wells and their prominent place in the life of the community, miracles that occurred related to water, important rivers and lakes, the use of water in baptisms, and the need for swimming lessons.

41. Fourteen Water Miracles

1. "Moses and Aaron did so, as the Lord commanded; and he lifted up the rod, and smote the waters that were in the river . . . and all the waters that were in the river were turned to blood" (Ex. 7:20).
2. While the Egyptian army pursued the children of Israel, the Lord opened a dry path across the Red Sea for the Israelites. The Egyptians followed closely behind the fleeing Hebrews but were drowned when the walls of water collapsed and filled the walkway (Ex. 14:21-29).
3. "When [the children of Israel] came to Marah, they could not drink of the waters of Marah, for they were bitter . . . and the people murmured against Moses, saying, What shall we drink? And he cried unto the Lord; and the Lord showed

him a tree, which when he had cast into the waters, the waters were made sweet" (Ex. 15:23-25).

4. In the desert the Israelites twice complained about having no water. Both times the Lord caused water to come out of a rock (Ex. 17:1-6; 20:1-11).

5. The waters of the Jordan rose up in a heap far upstream when the priests carrying the Ark of the Covenant dipped the soles of their feet into the water. The Israelites crossed the river on dry ground (Josh. 3:7-17).

6. Gideon wrung out a bowlful of water from the fleece in answer to prayer (Judges 6:38).

7. Elijah struck the waters of the Jordan with his mantle and he walked across on dry ground with Elisha. Elisha returned later with the same mantle and struck the waters. He crossed again on dry ground (2 Kings 2:8-14).

8. Elisha "healed" Jericho's water supply by throwing salt into it (2 Kings 2:19-22).

9. God gave water to the thirsty army of Israel by commanding them to dig trenches and then He filled them during the night without making it rain (2 Kings 3:14-22).

10. Naaman, commander of the Syrian army, was healed after dipping seven times in the Jordan River (2 Kings 5:14).

11. "As one was felling a beam, the axe head fell into the water: and he cried, and said, Alas, master! for it was borrowed. And [Elisha] said, Where fell it? And he showed him the place. And he cut down a stick, and cast it in thither; and the iron did swim . . . and he put out his hand and took it" (2 Kings 6:5-7).

12. Jesus walked on the Sea of Galilee to meet His disciples in their ship. Peter crawled over the side to join Him, and he also walked on the water (Matt. 14:25-31).

13. Jesus spoke to the sea and calmed it (Mark 4:39).

14. Jesus turned the water into wine at the wedding feast in Cana (John 2:1-10).

42. Eight Important Water Containers

1. "[Abraham's] servant ran to meet her [Rebekah], and said, Let me, I pray thee, drink a little water of thy *pitcher*. And she said, Drink, my lord: and . . . when she had done giving him drink, she said, I will draw water for thy camels also" (Gen. 24:17-19).

David's men at the well of Bethlehem

2. "The Lord spake unto Moses, saying, Thou shalt also make a *laver* of brass, and his foot also of brass, to wash withal: and thou shalt put it between the tabernacle of the congregation and the altar, and thou shalt put water therein. For Aaron and his sons shall wash their hands and their feet thereat" (Ex. 30:17-19).

3. Gideon set out a fleece of wool on the threshing floor. In the morning, though the ground around it was dry, he wrung a *bowl* of water from the fleece (Judges 6:36-38).

4. David sneaked into Saul's camp and took Saul's spear and *cruse* of water (1 Sam. 26:7-11).

5. After the priests of Baal failed to call down fire upon their sacrifice, Elijah built his altar to the Lord and had four *barrels* of water poured over the sacrifice three times (2 Kings 18:31-38).

6. "[Jesus'] disciples said unto him, Where wilt thou that we go and prepare that thou mayest eat the passover? And he sendeth forth two of his disciples, and saith unto them, Go

ye into the city, and there shall meet you a man bearing a *pitcher* of water: follow him" (Mark 14:12,13).

7. Jesus turned the water in six *waterpots* of stone into wine at Cana (John 2:6).
8. Jesus filled a *basin* with water and washed the disciples' feet (John 13:3-5).

43. Twelve Important Wells

1. The angel of the Lord spoke to Hagar at the well called Beer-lahai-roi between Kadesh and Bered (Gen. 16:7-14).
2. Abimelech's servants attempted to take a well called Beer-sheba away from Abraham. They settled their differences by making a covenant with one another (Gen. 21:22-32).
3. Abraham's servant found a wife for Isaac by the well at the city of Nahor (Gen. 24:10-67).
4. Isaac's servants dug two wells that he gave up to other herdsmen rather than fighting over them. He called them Esek and Sitnah. They then dug two more wells that he kept without trouble. He called them Rehoboth and Beer-sheba (Gen. 26:17-33).
5. Jacob met Rachel when she came to water her sheep at a well which was covered by a stone (Gen. 29:1-12).
6. Moses met his wife Zipporah when he helped her and her sisters water their flock at a well in the land of Midian (Ex. 2:15-21).
7. It was at the well of Harod that God whittled Gideon's troops down to the courageous three hundred (Judges 7:1-7).
8. After Samson slew a thousand men with the jawbone of an ass, he was extremely thirsty. God opened the ground and water came out. Samson called the well En-hakkore (Judges 15:18-20).
9. Abner was at the well of Sirah when he was summoned to his death by Joab's vigilantes (2 Sam. 3:26,27).
10. Jonathan and Ahimaaz escaped Absalom's men by hiding in a well in Bahurim (2 Sam. 17:17-21).
11. David longed for a drink from the well at Bethlehem, so three mighty men broke through the Philistine defenses and drew water for him. He poured it out as a sacrifice to the Lord (2 Sam. 23:14-17).
12. Jesus talked with the woman of Samaria at Jacob's well (John 4:5-15).

Pharaoh's army being drowned in the Red Sea

44. Thirteen Important Rivers, Brooks, Lakes, and Seas

1. A great river flowed into the Garden of Eden and divided into the *Pison,* the *Gihon,* the *Hiddekel,* and the *Euphrates* (Gen. 2:10-14).
2. The whole earth was covered by one huge sea during the Flood (Gen. 7:17-24).
3. The *Dead Sea* is called the *Salt Sea* in Gen. 14:3.
4. "The Lord made a covenant with Abram, saying, Unto thy seed have I given this land, from the *river of Egypt* unto the great river, the river *Euphrates*" (Gen. 15:18).
5. The first plague that God sent upon the Egyptians turned the waters of the *Nile River* to blood (Ex. 7:17-25).
6. Pharaoh and his men were drowned in the *Red Sea* after the Israelites had crossed over it on dry ground (Ex. 15:4).
7. The Promised Land bordered on the *great sea* (Num. 34:6),

also called the *sea of the Philistines* (Ex. 23:31), the *sea of Joppa* (Ezra 3:7), and the *sea of Cilicia* (Acts 27:5). We know it today as the *Mediterranean Sea.*

8. The Israelites crossed the *Jordan River* when they entered the Promised Land (Josh. 1:1,2).
9. David fled across the *brook Kidron* in his escape from Absalom (2 Sam. 15:13-23).
10. Elijah lived by the *brook Cherith* during the years of drought (1 Kings 17:1-4).
11. Ezra proclaimed a fast at the river *Ahava* (Ezra 8:21).
12. Jesus taught by the *lake of Gennesaret*—or *Galilee,* as we know it today (Luke 5:1-3).
13. John saw the *pure river of water of life* (Rev. 22:1).

45. Famous Swimmers

1. An iron axhead swam (2 Kings 6:5,6).
2. Peter swam to shore to meet Jesus (John 21:7-11).
3. Paul and 275 other people swam to shore or floated safely on broken pieces of their damaged ship (Acts 27:43,44).

46. Eleven Famous Baptisms

1. "Then cometh Jesus from Galilee to Jordan unto John, to be baptized of him" (Matt. 3:13).
2. Peter and the other disciples baptized about 3,000 people on the day of Pentecost (Acts 2:41).
3. Simon the sorcerer and others from Samaria were baptized by Philip (Acts 8:12,13).
4. "[The Ethiopian eunuch] commanded the chariot to stand still: and they went down both into the water, both Philip and the eunuch; and he baptized him" (Acts 8:38).
5. Paul was baptized by Ananias in Damascus (Acts 9:18).
6. Peter baptized Cornelius and his friends (Acts 10:23-48).
7. Lydia and her household were baptized by Paul and Silas (Acts 16:14,15).
8. The Philippian jailor took Paul and Silas to his home where they baptized him and his household (Acts 16:26-33).
9. "Crispus, the chief ruler of the synagogue, believed on the Lord with all his house; and many of the Corinthians hearing believed, and were baptized" (Acts 18:8).
10. Paul baptized about twelve Ephesian believers who had known only John's baptism (Acts 19:1-7).

11. "Moreover, brethren, I would not that ye should be ignorant, how that all our fathers were under the cloud, and all
passed through the sea; and were all baptized unto Moses
in the cloud and in the sea" (1 Cor. 10:1,2).

47. Three Drownings

1. "Fifteen cubits upward did the waters prevail; and the mountains were covered. And all flesh died that moved upon the
earth, both of fowl, and of cattle, and of beast, and of every
creeping thing that creepeth upon the earth, and every man:
all in whose nostrils was the breath of life, of all that was
in the dry land, died . . . and Noah only remained alive, and
they that were with him in the ark" (Gen. 7:20-23).
2. "The Lord is a man of war: the Lord is his name. Pharoah's
chariots and his host hath he cast into the sea: his chosen
captains also are drowned in the Red sea" (Ex. 15:3,4).
3. "And the unclean spirits went out, and entered into the
swine: and the herd ran violently down a steep place into
the sea, (they were about two thousand;) and were choked
in the sea" (Mark 5:13).

6

Questions

"Why, Daddy?" "Mommy, how do I do this?" "What is that?" "Why, how and what" seem to be the only words that a two-year-old knows. Even the most patient parent is tested by this incessant bombardment. Yet, by asking questions the child learns about life and its many facets.

Macaulay wrote: "Knowledge advances by steps and not by leaps." As we mature, we may ask fewer questions, but the three-word vocabulary remains very central. If we are going to continue learning about life, we will have to continue asking questions. Questions are stepping-stones to obtain knowledge.

God asks people questions and people ask God questions. Throughout the next seven lists, we find people wanting answers from God, and God questioning people to make them face the truth about their lives. God, of course, already knows the answer, but the person may be trying to cover the truth. In these lists you may find some questions you'd like to ask God; then again, you may find God asking you some questions.

48. Twenty-four Questions the Disciples Asked Jesus

1. "The disciples came and said unto [Jesus], Why speakest thou unto [the multitudes] in parables?" (Matt. 13:10).
2. Jesus "said unto them, Hear, and understand: not that which goeth into the mouth defileth a man; but that which cometh out of the mouth, this defileth a man. Then came [Jesus'] disciples, and said unto him, knowest thou that the Phari-

sees were offended, after they heard this saying?" (Matt. 15:10-12).

3. "Jesus called his disciples unto him, and said, I have compassion on the multitude.... And his disciples say unto him, Whence should we have so much bread in the wilderness, as to fill so great a multitude?" (Matt. 15:32,33).

4. Jesus' disciples asked Him, "Why then say the scribes that Elias must first come?" (Matt. 17:10).

5. "Jesus rebuked the devil; and he departed out of him: and the child was cured from that very hour. Then came the disciples to Jesus apart, and said, Why could not we cast him out?" (Matt. 17:14-19).

6. "The disciples [came] unto Jesus, saying, Who is the greatest in the kingdom of heaven?" (Matt. 18:1).

7. Peter came to Jesus, "and said, Lord, how oft shall my brother sin against me, and I forgive him? till seven times?" (Matt. 18:21).

8. "Then said Jesus unto his disciples, ... It is easier for a camel to go through the eye of a needle, than for a rich man to enter into the kingdom of God. When his disciples heard it, they were exceedingly amazed, saying, Who then can be saved?" (Matt. 19:23-25).

9. Peter asked Jesus, "Behold, we have forsaken all, and followed thee; what shall we have therefore?" (Matt. 19:27).

10. The disciples came to Jesus privately and asked, "When shall these things be? and what shall be the sign of thy coming, and of the end of the world?" (Matt. 24:3).

11. "Now the first day of the feast of unleavened bread the disciples came to Jesus, saying unto him, Where wilt thou that we prepare for thee to eat the passover?" (Matt. 26:6-9).

12. Jesus said, "Verily I say unto you, that one of you shall betray me. And they were exceedingly sorrowful, and began every one of them to say unto him, Lord, is it I?" (Matt. 26:21,22).

13. Jesus' disciples asked Him, "What might this parable [of the sower] be?" (Luke 8:9).

14. When James and John saw that the Samaritans did not receive Jesus, "they said, Lord, wilt thou that we command fire to come down from heaven, and consume them, even as Elias did?" (Luke 9:53,54).

15. Jesus said, "Be ye therefore ready also: for the Son of man

cometh at an hour when ye think not. Then Peter said unto him, Lord, speakest thou this parable unto us, or even to all?" (Luke 12:39-41).

16. Jesus said to the disciples, "Two men shall be in the field; the one shall be taken, and the other left. And they answered and said unto him, Where Lord?" (Luke 17:34-37).

17. Many of Jesus' disciples, when they heard about eating Jesus' flesh and drinking His blood said, "This is a hard saying; who can hear it?" (John 6:60).

18. "As Jesus passed by, he saw a man which was blind from his birth. And his disciples asked him, saying, Master, who did sin, this man, or his parents, that he was born blind?" (John 9:1,2).

19. Jesus said to His disciples, "Let us go into Judaea again. His disciples say unto him, Master, the Jews of late sought to stone thee; and goest thou thither again?" (John 11:7,8).

20. Jesus began to wash His disciples' feet. When He came to Peter, "Peter saith unto him, Lord, dost thou wash my feet?" (John 13:3-6).

21. Jesus said, "Whither I go, ye cannot come; . . . Simon Peter said unto him, Lord, whither goest thou?" (John 13:33,36).

22. Peter asked Jesus, "Lord, why cannot I follow thee now?" (John 13:37).

23. Thomas asked Jesus, "Lord, we know not whither thou goest; and how can we know the way?" (John 14:1-5).

24. "Judas saith unto [Jesus], not Iscariot, Lord, how is it that thou wilt manifest thyself unto us, and not unto the world?" (John 14:22).

49. Eighteen Questions the Religious Leaders Asked Jesus

1. "And they asked [Jesus], saying, Is it lawful to heal on the sabbath days?" (Matt. 12:10).

2. "Then came to Jesus scribes and Pharisees, which were of Jerusalem, saying, Why do thy disciples transgress the tradition of the elders? for they wash not their hands when they eat bread" (Matt. 15:1,2).

3. "The Pharisees also came unto Jesus, tempting him, and saying unto him, Is it lawful for a man to put away his wife for every cause?" (Matt. 19:3).

4. The Pharisees asked Jesus, "Why did Moses then command

to give a writing of divorcement, and to put her away?" (Matt. 19:7).

5. "When the chief priests and scribes saw the wonderful things that Jesus did, and the children crying in the temple, and saying, Hosanna to the son of David; they were sore displeased, and said unto him, Hearest what these say?" (Matt. 21:15,16).

6. While Jesus was in the temple teaching, the chief priests and the elders came to him and asked, "By what authority doest thou these things: and who gave thee this authority?" (Matt. 21:23).

7. The Pharisees sent men to Jesus to gather evidence against Him and they asked, "What thinkest thou? Is it lawful to give tribute to Caesar, or not?" (Matt. 22:15-17).

8. The Sadducees asked Jesus, "Now there were with us seven brethren: and the first, when he had married a wife, deceased, and, having no issue, left his wife unto his brother: likewise the second also, and the third, unto the seventh. And last of all the woman died also. Therefore in the resurrection whose wife shall she be of the seven? for they all had her" (Matt. 22:23-28).

9. A lawyer asked Jesus, "Master, which is the great commandment in the law?" (Matt. 22:35-36).

10. Jesus' disciples walked through a grain field an the Sabbath and plucked some heads of grain. The Pharisees asked Jesus, "Behold, why do they on the sabbath that which is not lawful?" (Mark 2:23,24).

11. "A certain lawyer stood up, and tempted [Jesus], saying, Master, what shall I do to inherit eternal life?" (Luke 10:25).

12. Jesus told a lawyer that he must love his neighbor as himself. "But he, willing to justify himself, said unto Jesus, And who is my neighbour?" (Luke 10:29).

13. After Jesus had chased the moneychangers out of the temple, the Jews asked Him, "What sign shewest thou unto us, seeing that thou doest these things?" (John 2:13-18).

14. "Nicodemus saith unto him, How can a man be born when he is old? can he enter the second time into his mother's womb and be born?" (John 3:3,4).

15. The scribes and Pharisees brought a woman caught in adultery to Jesus and they asked Him, "Now Moses in the law commanded us, that such should be stoned: but what sayest thou? This they said tempting him, that they might have to accuse him" (John 8:3-6).

16. Jesus said that the Father bore witness of Him. The Pharisees asked, "Where is thy Father?" (John 8:17-19).
17. The Pharisees asked Jesus, "Who art thou?" (John 8:25).
18. "Jesus said, For judgment I am come into this world, that they which see not might see; and that they which see might be made blind. And some of the Pharisees which were with him heard these words, and said unto him, Are we blind also?" (John 9:39,40).

50. Seven Questions Which Received No Answer

1. "Elijah asked the people of Israel, "How long halt ye between two opinions? If the Lord be God, follow him: but if Baal, then follow him. And the people answered him not a word" (1 Kings 18:21).
2. The King of Assyria sent his ambassador to King Hezekiah and asked him, "Who are [the gods of Samaria] among all the gods of these lands, that have delivered their land [into] my hand, that the Lord should deliver Jerusalem out of my hand? But they held their peace, and answered him not a word" (2 Kings 18:35,36).
3. The bride asked the city watchman, "Have you seen him whom my soul loves?" (Song of Sol. 3:3).
4. "Pilate asked Jesus again, saying, Answerest thou nothing? behold how many things they witness against thee. But Jesus answered nothing" (Mark 15:4,5).
5. "Jesus cried with a loud voice, saying, . . . My God, my God, why hast thou forsaken me?" (Mark 15:34).
6. "Then [Herod] questioned with him in many words; but he answered him nothing" (Luke 23:9).
7. "Pilate sayeth unto [Jesus], What is truth?" (John 18:38).

51. Twenty-five Questions People Asked God

1. Cain asked God, "Am I my brother's keeper?" (Gen. 4:9).
2. "Abram said, Lord God, what wilt thou give me, seeing I go childless, and the steward of my house is this Eliezer of Damascus?" (Gen. 15:2).
3. God said to Abram, "I am the Lord that brought thee out of Ur of the Chaldees, to give thee this land to inherit it. And he said, Lord God, whereby shall I know that I shall inherit it?" (Gen. 15:7,8).

4. Abraham questioned God about the destruction of Sodom without separating the righteous from the wicked and asked, "Shall not the Judge of all the earth do right?" (Gen. 18:25).

5. Abimelech had taken Sarah as his wife, but God showed him that she was actually Abraham's wife. He prayed for mercy and said, "Lord, wilt thou slay also a righteous nation?" (Gen. 20:4).

6. God called Moses to go to Pharaoh and release the Israelites, but Moses said, "Who am I, that I should go unto Pharaoh, and that I should bring forth the children of Israel out of Egypt?" (Ex. 3:10,11).

7. "Moses said unto God, Behold, when I come unto the children of Israel, and shall say unto them, The God of your fathers hath sent me unto you; and they shall say to me, What is his name? what shall I say unto them?" (Ex. 3:13).

8. After Moses' first failure to convince Pharaoh to let Israel go, "Moses returned unto the Lord, and said, Lord, wherefore hast thou so evil entreated this people? why is it that thou hast sent me?" (Ex. 5:22).

9. God commanded Moses to go back to Pharaoh, but Moses balked and said, "Behold, the children of Israel have not hearkened unto me; how then shall Pharaoh hear me, who am of uncircumcised lips?" (Ex. 6:12).

10. The people murmured against Moses "and Moses cried unto the Lord, saying, What shall I do unto this people? they be almost ready to stone me" (Ex. 17:3,4).

11. Moses pleaded with God not to destroy the Israelites, praying, "Wherefore should the Egyptians speak, and say, For mischief did he bring them out, to slay them in the mountains, and to consume them from the face of the earth?" (Ex. 32:12).

12. Moses asked God, "Wherein shall it be known here that I and thy people have found grace in thy sight? is it not that thou goest with us?" (Ex. 33:16).

13. The Israelites cried to Moses for meat, "and Moses said unto the Lord, Wherefore hast thou afflicted thy servant? and wherefore have I not found favour in thy sight, that thou layest the burden of all this people upon me?" (Num. 11:11).

14. Korah had rebelled against the authority of Moses, and God was about to destroy him. Moses and Aaron, fearing for the rest of the people, cried, "O God, the God of the spirits of

all flesh, shall one man sin, and wilt thou be wroth with all the congregation?" (Num 16:22).

15. After Israel lost their first battle against Ai, "Joshua said, Alas O Lord God, wherefore hast thou at all brought this people over Jordan, to deliver us into the hand of the Amorites, to destroy us?" (Josh. 7:7).

16. "Now after the death of Joshua it came to pass, that the children of Israel asked the Lord, saying, Who shall go up for us against the Canaanites first, to fight against them?" (Judges 1:1).

17. After nearly exterminating the tribe of Benjamin, the Israelites prayed, "O Lord God of Israel, why is this come to pass in Israel, that there should be today one tribe lacking in Israel?" (Judges 21:2,3).

18. The Philistines were plundering Keilah. "Therefore David inquired of the Lord, saying, Shall I go and smite these Philistines?" (1 Sam. 23:1,2).

19. After the Amalekites had taken Ziklag and had carried away the inhabitants, "David inquired at the Lord, saying, Shall I pursue after this troop? shall I overtake them?" (1 Sam. 30:3-8).

20. Solomon prayed, "Give therefore thy servant an understanding heart to judge thy people, that I may discern between good and bad: for who is able to judge this thy so great a people?" (1 Kings 3:5-9).

21. Elijah cried to the Lord, "and said, O Lord my God, hast thou also brought evil upon the widow with whom I sojourn, by slaying her son?" (1 Kings 17:20).

22. Job answered the Lord in response to a long list of hard questions "and said, Behold, I am vile; what shall I answer thee?" (Job 40:3,4).

23. Jeremiah cried to God, "Why is my pain perpetual, and my wound incurable, which refuseth to be healed? wilt thou be altogether unto me as a liar, and as waters that fail?" (Jer. 15:18).

24. Ezekiel fell on his face, "and cried with a loud voice, and said, Ah Lord God! wilt thou make a full end of the remnant of Israel?" (Ezek. 11:13).

25. "The burden which Habakkuk the prophet did see. O Lord, how long shall I cry, and thou wilt not hear! . . . Why dost thou shew me iniquity, and cause me to behold grievance?" (Hab. 1:1-3).

52. Forty-five Questions God Asked People

1. When Adam and Eve had sinned, they hid from the presence of God "and the Lord God called unto Adam, and said unto him, Where art thou?" (Gen. 3:6-9).

2. The Lord asked Adam, "Who told thee that thou wast naked? Hast thou eaten of the tree, whereof I commanded thee that thou shouldest not eat?" (Gen. 3:11).

3. "And the Lord God said unto the woman, What is this that thou hast done?" (Gen. 3:13).

4. After Cain's offering was rejected by God, "Cain was very wroth, and his countenance fell. And the Lord said unto Cain, Why art thou wroth? and why is thy countenance fallen? If thou doest well, shalt thou not be accepted?" (Gen. 4:6-7).

5. "Cain rose up against Abel his brother, and slew him. And the Lord said unto Cain, Where is Abel thy brother? . . . What hast thou done?" (Gen 4:8-10).

6. "The Lord said unto Abraham, Wherefore did Sarah laugh, saying, Shall I of a surety bear a child, which am old? Is anything too hard for the Lord?" (Gen. 18:13).

7. "The Lord said unto [Moses], What is that in thine hand?" (Ex. 4:2).

8. "Moses said unto the Lord, O my Lord, I am not eloquent, . . . And the Lord said unto him, Who hath made man's mouth?" (Ex. 4:10,11).

9. As Pharaoh's army approached, the people cried to Moses, "and the Lord said unto Moses, Wherefore criest thou unto me?" (Ex. 14:15).

10. The Israelites questioned God's provision of manna for the Sabbath. "And the Lord said unto Moses, How long refuse ye to keep my commandments and my laws?" (Ex. 16:27,28).

11. Moses asked the Lord how he was to get the meat that the people demanded, and "the Lord said unto Moses, Is the Lord's hand waxed short? thou shalt see whether my word shall come to pass or not" (Num. 11:23).

12. Aaron and Miriam criticized Moses, and God said, "With him will I speak mouth to mouth, . . . wherefore then were ye not afraid to speak against my servant Moses?" (Num. 12:8).

13. Moses asked the Lord to lift the judgment of leprosy from Miriam "and the Lord said unto Moses, If her father had

Cain after Abel's murder

but spit in her face, should she not be ashamed seven days?"
(Num. 12:13,14).

14. When the children of Israel refused to go into the Promised
Land, "the Lord said unto Moses, How long will this people
provoke me?" (Num. 14:11).

15. After Moses had died, God asked Joshua, "Have not I commanded thee? Be strong and of good courage; be not afraid,
neither be thou dismayed" (Josh. 1:1,9).

16. "The Lord said unto Samuel, How long wilt thou mourn for
Saul, seeing I have rejected him from reigning over Israel?"
(1 Sam. 16:1).

17. "The word of the Lord came unto Nathan, saying, Go and
tell my servant David, Thus saith the Lord, Shalt thou build
me an house for me to dwell in?" (2 Sam. 7:4,5).

18. After David had engineered the death of Uriah, God spoke to him through Nathan and said, "Wherefore hast thou despised the commandment of the Lord, to do evil in his sight?" (2 Sam. 12:9).

19. After David had sinned by numbering Israel and Judah, God offered him a choice of judgments, asking, "Shall seven years of famine come unto thee in thy land? or wilt thou flee three months before thine enemies, while they pursue thee? or that there be three days' pestilence in thy land?" (2 Sam. 24:13).

20. After Elijah ran away from Jezebel, he came to a cave, and "behold, the word of the Lord came to him, and he said unto him, What doest thou here, Elijah?" (1 Kings 19:9).

21. When Ahab had taken Naboth's vineyard, God sent Elijah, "saying, Thus saith the Lord, Hast thou killed, and also taken possession?" (1 Kings 21:19).

22. After Elijah had rebuked Ahab, God asked Elijah, "Seest thou how Ahab humbleth himself before me?" (1 Kings 21:29).

23. Isaiah "heard the voice of the Lord, saying, Whom shall I send, and who will go for us?" (Isa. 6:8).

24. "Is there a God beside me?" (Isa. 44:8).

25. The Lord asked Cyrus, "Shall the clay say to him that fashioneth it, What makest thou?" (Isa. 45:1-9).

26. "Is my hand shortened at all, that it cannot redeem? or have I no power to deliver?" (Isa. 50:2).

27. Jeremiah cried out in the temple, "Is this house, which is called by my name, become a den of robbers in your eyes? Behold, even I have seen it, saith the Lord" (Jer. 7:11).

28. The Lord asked, "Why is this people of Jerusalem slidden back by a perpetual backsliding?" (Jer. 8:4-12).

29. "Am I a God at hand, saith the Lord, and not a God afar off? Can any hide himself in secret places that I shall not see him? saith the Lord. Do not I fill heaven and earth? saith the Lord" (Jer. 23:23,24).

30. "Then came the word of the Lord unto Jeremiah, saying, Behold, I am the Lord, the God of all flesh: is there anything too hard for me?" (Jer. 32:26,27).

31. "Thus saith the Lord, the God of Israel, unto thee, O Baruch; . . . Seekest thou great things for thyself? seek them not" (Jer. 45:2,5).

32. Ezekiel prophesied against the false prophets of Israel

saying, "Have ye not seen a vain vision, and have ye not spoken a lying divination, whereas ye say, The Lord saith it; albeit I have not spoken?" (Ezek. 13:7).

33. Several Elders of Israel came to Ezekiel and God said, "Son of man, these men have set up their idols in their heart, and put the stumbling-block of their iniquity before their face: should I be inquired of at all by them?" (Ezek. 14:1-3).

34. "Have I any pleasure at all that the wicked should die? saith the Lord God: and not that he should return from his ways, and live?" (Ezek. 18:23).

35. The Lord asked Israel, "Can thine heart endure, or can thine hands be strong, in the days that I shall deal with thee?" (Ezek. 22:14).

36. Ezekiel prophesied against Israel, "Thus saith the Lord God; Ye eat with the blood, and lift up your eyes toward your idols, and shed blood: and shall ye possess the land?" (Ezek. 33:25).

37. God showed Ezekiel a valley of dry bones and asked him, "Son of man, can these bones live?" (Ezek. 37:3).

38. The Lord asked Israel, "Shall a trumpet be blown in the city, and the people not be afraid? shall there be evil in a city, and the Lord hath not done it?" (Amos 3:6).

39. Jonah was angry about his gourd that had died. "Then said the Lord, Doest thou well to be angry?" (Jonah 4:9).

40. The Lord asked Jonah, "Should not I spare Nineveh, that great city, wherein are more than sixscore thousand persons that cannot discern between their right hand and their left hand; and also much cattle?" (Jonah 4:11).

41. "Thus saith the Lord of hosts; Ask now the priests concerning the law, saying, If one bear holy flesh in the skirt of his garment, and with his skirt do touch bread, or pottage, or wine, or oil, or any meat, shall it be holy?" (Hag. 2:11,12).

42. Zechariah prophesied to the people and the priests, saying, "When ye fasted and mourned in the fifth and seventh month, even those seventy years, did ye at all fast unto me?" (Zech. 7:4-6).

43. "A son honoureth his father, and a servant his master: if then I be a father, where is mine honour? and if I be a master where is my fear? saith the Lord of hosts unto you, O priests, that despise my name" (Mal. 1:6).

44. Malachi spoke forth the word of the Lord, asking, "If ye offer the blind sacrifice, is it not evil? and if ye offer the

lame and sick, is it not evil? offer it now unto thy governor; will he be pleased with thee, or accept thy person?" (Mal. 1:8).

45. God pleaded for Israel to tithe, asking, "Will a man rob God?" (Mal. 3:8).

53. Thirty-four Questions God Asked Job

1. "Who is this that darkeneth counsel by words without knowledge?" (Job 38:2).
2. "Gird up now thy loins like a man; for I will demand of thee, and answer thou me. Where wast thou when I laid the foundations of the earth?" (Job 38:3,4).
3. "Who shut up the sea with doors, when it brake forth, as if it had issued out of the womb?" (Job 38:8).
4. "Hast thou commanded the morning since thy days; and caused the day-spring to know his place; that it might take hold of the ends of the earth, that the wicked might be shaken out of it?" (Job 38:12,13).
5. "Hast thou entered into the springs of the sea? or hast thou walked in the search of the depth?" (Job 38:16).
6. "Have the gates of death been opened unto thee? or hast thou seen the doors of the shadow of death?" (Job 38:17).
7. "Hast thou perceived the breadth of the earth?" (Job 38:18).
8. "Where is the way where light dwelleth? and as for darkness, where is the place thereof, that thou shouldest take it to the bound thereof, and that thou shouldest know the paths to the house thereof?" (Job 38:19,20).
9. "Hast thou entered into the treasures of the snow? or hast thou seen the treasures of the hail, which I have reserved against the time of trouble, against the day of battle and war?" (Job 38:22,23).
10. "By what way is the light parted, which scattereth the east wind upon the earth?" (Job 38:24).
11. "Who hath divided a watercourse for the overflowing of waters, or a way for the lightning of thunder; to cause it to rain on the earth, where no man is; on the wilderness, wherein there is no man; to satisfy the desolate and waste ground; and to cause the bud of the tender herb to spring forth?" (Job 38:25-27).
12. "Hath the rain a father? or who hath begotten the drops of dew?" (Job 38:28).

13. "Out of whose womb came the ice? and the hoary frost of heaven, who hath gendered it?" (Job 38:29).
14. "Canst thou bind the sweet influences of Pleiades, or loose the bands of Orion? Canst thou bring forth Mazzaroth in his season? or canst thou guide Arcturus with his sons?" (Job 38:31,32).
15. "Knowest thou the ordinances of heaven? canst thou set the dominion thereof in the earth?" (Job 38:33).
16. "Canst thou lift up thy voice to the clouds, that abundance of waters may cover thee?" (Job 38:34).
17. "Canst thou send lightnings, that they may go, and say unto thee, Here we are?" (Job 38:35).
18. "Who hath put wisdom in the inward parts? or who hath given understanding to the heart?" (Job 38:36).
19. "Who can number the clouds in wisdom? or who can stay the bottles of heaven, when the dust groweth into hardness, and the clods cleave fast together?" (Job 38:37,38).
20. "Wilt thou hunt the prey for the lion? or fill the appetite of the young lions, when they couch in their dens, and abide in the covert to lie in wait?" (Job 38:39,40).
21. "Who provideth for the raven his food?" (Job 38:41).
22. "Knowest thou the time when the wild goats of the rock bring forth? or canst thou mark when the hinds do calve?" (Job 39:1).
23. "Who hath sent out the wild ass free? or who hath loosed the bands of the wild ass?" (Job 39:5).
24. "Canst thou bind the unicorn with his band in the furrow? or will he harrow the valleys after thee? Wilt thou trust him, because his strength is great?" (Job 39:10,11).
25. "Gavest thou the goodly wings unto the peacocks? or wings and feathers unto the ostrich?" (Job 39:13).
26. "Hast thou given the horse strength? hast thou clothed his neck with thunder? Canst thou make him afraid as a grass-hopper?" (Job 39:19,20).
27. "Doth the hawk fly by thy wisdom, and stretch her wings toward the south?" (Job 39:26).
28. "Doth the eagle mount up at thy command, and make her nest on high?" (Job 39:27).
29. "Moreover the Lord answered Job, and said, Shall he that contendeth with the Almighty instruct him? he that re-proveth God, let him answer it" (Job 40:1,2).
30. "Wilt thou also disannul my judgment? wilt thou condemn me, that thou mayest be righteous?" (Job 40:8).

31. "Hast thou an arm like God? or canst thou thunder with a voice like him?" (Job 40:9).
32. "Canst thou draw out leviathan with an hook? or his tongue with a cord which thou lettest down? Canst thou put an hook into his nose?" (Job 41:1,2).
33. "None is so fierce that dare stir [leviathan] up: who then is able to stand before me?" (Job 41:10).
34. "Who hath prevented me, that I should repay him? whatsoever is under the whole heaven is mine" (Job 41:11).

54. Forty-six Questions Jesus Asked People

1. Clarifying our need for a single heart: "If therefore the light that is in thee be darkness, how great is the darkness!" (Matt. 6:23).
2. When speaking about God's ability to provide, Jesus asked His disciples, "Why take ye thought for raiment . . . shall he not much more clothe you, O ye of little faith?" (Matt. 6:28-30).
3. "Why beholdest thou the mote that is in thy brother's eye, but considerest not the beam that is in thine own eye?" (Matt. 7:3).
4. "How much more shall your Father which is in heaven give good things to them that ask him?" (Matt. 7:11).
5. When the disciples were afraid the storm would sink their boat, Jesus asked, "Why are ye fearful, O ye of little faith?" (Matt. 8:26).
6. Jesus began to say unto the multitudes concerning John, "What went ye out into the wilderness to see?" (Matt. 11:7-10).
7. When Jesus spoke about removing a sheep from a pit on the Sabbath, He asked, "How much then is a man better than a sheep?" (Matt. 12:12).
8. To the Pharisees and scribes: "O generation of vipers, how can ye, being evil, speak good things?" (Matt. 12:34).
9. When confronted with feeding the multitude, Jesus asked the disciples, "How many loaves have ye?" (Matt. 15:34).
10. To a forgetful band of disciples: "Do ye not yet understand, neither remember the five loaves of the five thousand, and how many baskets ye took up?" (Matt. 16:9).
11. When speaking about discipleship, Jesus asked, "For what is a man profited, if he shall gain the whole world, and lose

his own soul? or what shall a man give in exchange for his soul?" (Matt. 16:26).

12. When the disciples were unable to deliver the boy possessed by the devil, Jesus asked, "O faithless and perverse generation, how long shall I be with you? how long shall I suffer you?" (Matt. 17:17).

13. "What thinkest thou, Simon? Of whom do the kings of the earth take custom or tribute? of their children, or of strangers?" (Matt. 17:25).

14. To the person who labeled Jesus good: "Why callest thou me good?" (Matt. 19:17).

15. When the mother of James and John desired her sons to be in a prominent role, Jesus asked her, "What wilt thou?" (Matt. 20:21).

16. Jesus to the two blind men: "What will ye that I shall do unto you?" (Matt. 20:32).

17. When challenged as to the source of his authority, Jesus countered the chief priests by asking, "The baptism of John, whence was it? from heaven, or of men?" (Matt. 21:25).

18. When beginning a parable, Jesus asked, "But what think ye?" (Matt. 21:28).

19. When questioned by the Pharisees, Jesus unmasked their request by asking, "Why tempt ye me, ye hypocrites?" (Matt. 22:18).

20. Jesus took the offensive and asked the Pharisees, "What think ye of Christ? whose son is he?" (Matt. 22:42).

21. Jesus asked the scribes and Pharisees, "Ye serpents, ye generation of vipers, how can ye escape the damnation of hell?" (Matt. 23:33).

22. When His disciples questioned the woman about wasting the ointment on Jesus, He asked them, "Why trouble ye the woman?" (Matt. 26:10).

23. When the disciples fell asleep before Jesus was betrayed, He asked them, "What, could ye not watch with me one hour?" (Matt. 26:40).

24. To the scribes, who questioned Jesus' ability to forgive sins, He asked, "Why reason ye these things in your hearts?" (Mark 2:8).

25. To those who claimed that Jesus' power over demons came from Satan, He questioned, "How can Satan cast out Satan?" (Mark 3:23).

26. To the demoniac, "What is thy name?" (Mark 5:9).

27. To those who mourned the death of the ruler of the syno-gogue's daughter, "Why make ye this ado, and weep?" (Mark 5:39).

28. Deeply disturbed by the Pharisees tempting Him, Jesus asked, "Why doth this generation seek after a sign?" (Mark 8:12).

29. To the father whose son was demon possessed: "How long is it ago since this came unto him?" (Mark 9:21).

30. To the disciples who were discussing which of them was the greatest: "What was it that ye disputed among yourselves by the way?" (Mark 9:33).

31. To the Pharisees who were trying to find fault with Jesus' teaching: "What did Moses command you?" (Mark 10:3).

32. "My God, my God, why hast thou forsaken me?" (Mark 15:34).

33. "Why call ye me, Lord, Lord, and do not the things which I say?" (Luke 6:46).

34. "Ye hypocrites, ye can discern the face of the sky and of the earth; but how is it that ye do not discern this time?" (Luke 12:56).

35. To the inquiring of Nicodemus: "If I have told you earthly things, and ye believe not, how shall ye believe, if I tell you of heavenly things?" (John 3:12).

36. To the Jews whose trust was not rooted in God: "How can ye believe, which receive honour one of another and seek not the honour that cometh from God only?" (John 5:44).

37. When His disciples could not handle Jesus' teaching, Jesus asked them, "Doth this offend you?" (John 6:61).

38. Before a crowd of skeptical Jews He asked, "Did not Moses give you the law, and yet none of you keepeth the law? Why go ye about to kill me?" (John 7:19).

39. In challenging the Jewish belief that their heritage made them God's people: "Which of you convinceth me of sin? And if I say the truth, why do ye not believe me?" (John 8:46).

40. To His Father in heaven: "Now is my soul troubled; and what shall I say?" (John 12:27).

41. After washing the disciples' feet, "Know ye what I have done to you?" (John 13:12).

42. "Have I been so long time with you, and yet hast thou not known me, Philip?" (John 14:9).

43. To the officer who defended the high priest: "Why smitest thou me?" (John 18:23).

44. To Mary after His resurrection: "Woman, why weepest thou? whom seekest thou?" (John 20:15).

45. To a troubled, searching disciple: "Simon, son of Jonas, lovest thou me?" (John 21:17).

46. To a prostrating hater of the Church: "Saul, Saul, why persecutest thou me?" (Acts 9:4).

7

Decisions

Every day our lives are filled with decisions. Many decisions are routine (should I have juice for breakfast? etc.) and will not have a particularly profound effect. Others will have varying degrees of importance and impact upon us.

There is one decision, though, that ranks far above every other decision an individual faces: Am I going to obey God or not? Even our everyday decisions reflect whether we seek to glorify God or serve our own interests.

The following three lists demonstrate the impact of decisions in the lives of people in the Bible.

55. Ten Decisions to Follow God

1. Noah
   "Noah was a just man and perfect in his generations, and Noah walked with God. . . . And God said unto Noah, . . . Make thee an ark of gopher wood; . . . Thus did Noah; according to all that God commanded him, so did he" (Gen. 6:9,13,14,22).
2. Abraham
   "Now the Lord had said unto Abram, Get thee out of thy country, and from thy kindred, and from thy father's house, unto a land that I will shew thee . . . so Abram departed, as the Lord had spoken unto him" (Gen. 12:1,4).
3. Moses
   "And the Lord said unto Moses in Midian, Go, return into Egypt: for all the men are dead which sought thy life. And Moses took his wife and sons, and set them upon an ass, and

he returned to the land of Egypt: and Moses took the rod of God in his hand" (Ex. 4:19,20).

4. Israel

"[Joshua commanded] Choose you this day whom ye will serve; whether the gods which your fathers served that were on the other side of the flood, or the gods of the Amorites, in whose land ye dwell: but as for me and my house, we well serve the Lord. And the people answered and said, God forbid that we should forsake the Lord, to serve other gods ... we will serve the Lord" (Josh. 24:15,16,21).

5. King Josiah

"When the king had heard the words of the book of the law, he rent his clothes ... and made a covenant before the Lord to walk after the Lord, and to keep his commandments" (2 Kings 22:11; 23:3).

6. Daniel

"But Daniel purposed in his heart that he would not defile himself with the portion of the king's meat, nor with the wine which he drank" (Dan. 1:8).

7. Nebuchadnezzar

"And at the end of the days I Nebuchadnezzar lifted up mine eyes unto heaven, and mine understanding returned unto me, and I blessed the most High, and I praised and honoured him that liveth for ever, whose dominion is an everlasting dominion. ... At the same time my reason returned to me. ... Now I Nebuchadnezzar praise and extol and honour the King of heaven" (Dan. 4:34-37).

8. The king and the people of Nineveh

"So the people of Nineveh believed God, and proclaimed a fast, and put on sackcloth, from the greatest of them even to the least of them. For word came unto the king of Nineveh, and he arose from his throne, and he laid his robe from him, and covered him with sackcloth, and sat in ashes" (Jonah 3:5,6).

9. Peter and Andrew

"Jesus, walking by the sea of Galilee, saw two brethren, Simon called Peter, and Andrew his brother, casting a net into the sea: for they were fishers. And he saith unto them, Follow me, and I will make you fishers of men. And they straightway left their nets, and followed him" (Matt. 4:18-20).

10. The Philippian jailor
    "The jailor fell down before Paul and Silas, and brought
    them out, and said, Sirs, what must I do to be saved? ...
    When he had brought them into his house, he set meat
    before them, and rejoiced, believing in God with all his
    house" (Acts 16:29,30,34).

56. Ten Decisions to Serve the Devil

1. Eve
   "When the woman saw that the tree was good for food, and
   that it was pleasant to the eyes, and a tree to be desired to
   make one wise, she took of the fruit thereof, and did eat, and
   gave also unto her husband with her and he did eat" (Gen.
   3:6).

Jesus calls Simon and Andrew

72

2. Lot's wife
"But his wife looked back from behind him, and she became a pillar of salt" (Gen. 19:26).
3. Aaron and the people of Israel
"When the people saw that Moses delayed to come down out of the mount, the people gathered themselves together unto Aaron, and said unto him, Up, make us gods, which shall go before us ..." and Aaron did so (Ex. 32:1).
4. Solomon
"It came to pass, when Solomon was old, that his wives turned away his heart after other gods: and his heart was not perfect with the Lord his God, as was the heart of David his father" (1 Kings 11:4).
5. Jeroboam
"The king took counsel, and made two calves of gold, and said unto [Israel], It is too much for you to go up to Jerusalem: behold thy gods, O Israel, which brought thee up out of the land of Egypt" (1 Kings 12:28).
6. Ahab
"And it came to pass, as if it had been a light thing for [Ahab] to walk in the sins of Jeroboam the son of Nebat, that he took to wife Jezebel the daughter of Ethbaal king of the Zidonians, and went and served Baal, and worshipped him" (1 Kings 16:31).
7. Judas Iscariot
"Then entered Satan into Judas. . . . And he promised, and sought opportunity to betray [Jesus] unto them in the absence of the multitude" (Luke 22:3,6).
8. Ananias
"A certain man named Ananias, with Sapphira his wife, sold a possession, and kept back part of the price, his wife also being privy to it, and brought a certain part and laid it at the apostles' feet. But Peter said, Ananias, why hath Satan filled thine heart to lie to the Holy Ghost, and to keep back part of the price of the land?" (Acts 5:1-3).
9. Elymas
"Elymas the sorcerer ... withstood [Barnabas and Saul], seeking to turn away the deputy [Sergius Paulus] from the faith" (Acts 13:8).
10. Demas
"Demas hath forsaken me, having loved this present world" (2 Tim. 4:10).

57. Decisions and the Heart

1. "O that there were such an heart in them, that they would fear me, and keep all my commandments always" (Deut. 5:29).
2. "To prove thee, to know what was in thine heart, whether thou wouldst keep his commandments" (Deut. 8:2).
3. "Only fear the Lord, and serve him in truth with all your heart" (1 Sam. 12:24).
4. "The Lord was angry with Solomon, because his heart turned away from the Lord God of Israel" (1 Kings 11:9).
5. "I have walked before thee in truth and with perfect heart, and have done that which is good in thy sight" (2 Kings 20:3).
6. "Solomon my son, know thou the God of thy father, and serve him with a perfect heart and with a willing mind" (1 Chron. 28:9).
7. "The people rejoiced, for that they offered willingly, because with perfect heart they offered willingly to the Lord" (1 Chron. 29:9).
8. "Keep thy heart with all diligence; for out of it are the issues of life" (Prov. 4:23).
9. "The heart is deceitful above all things. . . . I the Lord search the heart, I try the reins, even to give every man according to his ways" (Jer. 17:9,10).
10. "Cast away from you all your transgressions, whereby ye have transgressed; and make you a new heart and a new spirit: for why will ye die?" (Ezek. 18:31).
11. "But Daniel purposed in his heart that he would not defile himself" (Dan. 1:8).
12. "For where your treasure is, there will your heart be also" (Matt. 6:21).
13. "A good man out of the good treasure of the heart bringeth forth good things" (Matt. 12:35).
14. "For from within, out of the heart of men, proceed evil thoughts, adulteries. . . . These evil things come from within, and defile the man" (Mark 7:21,23).
15. "That which fell on the good ground are they, which in an honest and good heart, having heard the word, keep it, and bring forth fruit with patience" (Luke 8:15).
16. To Simon the sorcerer: "Thou hast neither part nor lot in this matter: for thy heart is not right in the sight of God" (Acts 8:21).

17. "Ye have obeyed from the heart that form of doctrine which was delivered you" (Rom. 6:17).

18. "Harden not your hearts. . . . Take heed, brethren, lest there be in any of you an evil heart of unbelief, in departing from the living God" (Heb. 3:8,12).

19. "I am he which searcheth the reins and hearts: and I will give unto every one of you according to your works" (Rev. 2:23).

8

God's Personality

Devout Orientals speak of God as the all-pervading "Force" in the universe. On every continent there are people who think God is the sovereign "bogeyman" in every tree, rock and river. And in our culture, many people see God as an aloof old man who set the cosmos in motion, then retired to some deserted asteroid.

Happily, none of the above ideas is correct. In fact, *God is the most fascinating person in the universe.* And what makes God's personality most interesting is that *we* are similar to Him in many respects. We are able to reason, to create, to choose, to feel emotion, even as God is able to do these things. We must realize, of course, that He does all these perfectly, unlike our *human* attempts.

Because we are created in the image of God and because of his concern for us, we can speak to Him, listen to Him, and become more like Him in character. As you read the following lists, you may be surprised to learn what God is really like. And, hopefully, you will be aroused to study and better understand His personality.

58. Six Times God Expressed Contentment

1. God expresses His intense desire to find people to whom He can entrust himself: "For the eyes of the Lord run to and fro throughout the whole earth, to show himself strong in the behalf of them whose heart is perfect toward him" (2 Chron. 16:9).

2. God expresses His happiness in extending forgiveness: "He retaineth not his anger for ever, because he delighteth in

mercy. He will turn again, he will have compassion upon us" (Mic. 7:18-19).

3. God expresses His heart of joy over an obedient people: "The Lord thy God in the midst of thee is mighty; he will save, he will rejoice over thee with joy; he will rest in his love, he will joy over thee with singing" (Zeph. 3:17).

4. Jesus compared His Father's compassion and anger to a human lord: "The lord of that servant was moved with compassion, and loosed him, and forgave him the debt. . . . His lord was wroth. . . . So likewise shall my heavenly father do . . ." (Matt. 18:27,34,35).

5. The happiness of heaven can only be a reflection of the heart of God: "There is joy in the presence of the angels of God over one sinner that repenteth" (Luke 15:7,10).

6. An amazing revelation of God's desire for us: "For the Father seeketh such to worship him" (John 4:23).

59. Six Times God Expressed Disappointment

1. When sin ran rampant throughout mankind after the fall: "It repented the Lord that he had made man on earth, and it grieved him at his heart" (Gen. 6:5,6).

2. A historical view of the children of Israel: "For they provoked him to anger with their high places, and moved him to jealousy with their graven images. When God heard this, he was wroth, and greatly abhorred Israel" (Ps. 78:58,59).

3. The heart of God as He was so long-suffering with a disobedient people: "Forty years long was I grieved with this generation . . . unto whom I sware in my wrath that they should not enter my rest" (Ps. 95:10,11).

4. "Thou wast angry with me, thine anger is turned away, and thou comfortedst me" (Isa. 12:1).

5. "Because I am broken with their whorish heart" (Ezek. 6:9).

6. "I am jealous for Jerusalem and for Zion with a great jealousy. And I am very sore displeased with the heathen that are at ease: for I was but a little displeased, and they helped toward the affliction" (Zech. 1:14,15).

60. Thirteen Times God Revealed New Choices

1. "God said, Let us make man in our image, after our likeness" (Gen. 1:26).

2. "Therefore, the Lord sent him forth from the garden of Eden" (Gen. 3:23).
3. "It repented the Lord that he had made man on the earth" (Gen. 6:6).
4. God chose to destroy all mankind, except Noah and his family, because they were utterly corrupted (Gen. 6:12-13).
5. "I will establish my covenant with you; neither shall all flesh be cut off any more by the waters of a flood" (Gen. 9:11,12).
6. The Lord chose to withhold his anger and not destroy the rebellious children of Israel (Ex. 32:7-14,30-33).
7. King Hezekiah's seeking the Lord resulted in God's changing His decision and extending Hezekiah's life fifteen years (2 Kings 20:5,6).
8. "Even so the Son quickeneth whom he will" (John 5:21).
9. "I have power to lay it down, and I have power to take it again" (John 10:18).
10. "It is not for you to know the times or the seasons, which the Father hath put in his own power" (Acts 1:7).
11. "All these worketh that one and the self-same Spirit, dividing to every man severally as he will" (1 Cor. 12:11).
12. "Of his own will begat he us with the word of truth" (James 1:18).
13. "The Father sent the Son to be the Saviour of the world" (1 John 4:14).

61. Eight Times God Revealed His Thoughts

1. Moses by reasoning with the Lord staved off the wrath of God when Israel worshipped the golden calf (Ex. 32:7-14).
2. "I will raise up a faithful priest, that shall do according to that which is in mine heart and in my mind" (1 Sam. 2:35).
3. "Come now, and let us reason together, saith the Lord" (Isa. 1:18).
4. "Produce your cause, saith the Lord; bring forth your strong reasons, saith the King of Jacob" (Isa. 41:21).
5. "For my thoughts are not your thoughts. . . . As the heavens are higher than the earth, so are . . . my thoughts than your thoughts" (Isa. 55:8,9).
6. "For I know the thoughts that I think toward you, saith the Lord, thoughts of peace, and not of evil, to give you an expected end" (Jer. 29:11).
7. "Wherefore I will yet plead with you, saith the Lord, and with your children's children will I plead" (Jer. 2:1-13).

8. "For the Lord hath a controversy with his people, and he will plead with Israel. O my people, what have I done unto thee? and wherein have I wearied thee? testify against me" (Mic. 6:1-3).

62. Sixteen Times God Showed Flexibility in Dealing with Mankind

1. God regretted that man had been created. Here we find an aroused state of grief and disappointment over man's persistent rebellion (Gen. 6:3,5-7).
2. Here we have the amazing statement from God concerning the implications of Abraham's obedience: "For now I know that thou fearest God." A ram was provided in Isaac's place (Gen. 22:12).

The Ninevites repent

3. Here Moses' intercessions changed the mind of God to not destroy the nation of Israel (Ex. 32:7-14).

4. God was waiting to see Israel's reaction of humility after the golden-calf incident before determining His judgment upon them (Ex. 33:5).

5. Another of God's judgments was stayed by the humility and prayer of Moses (Num. 11:1,2).

6. God was using the forty years of wandering in the wilderness to discover Israel's true heart toward His rule (Deut. 8:2).

7. God decided not to drive out some of the nations in Palestine because of Israel's sin. They would be His instrument to test and prove Israel's faithfulness (Judges 2:20-22).

8. When Saul disobeyed God's directions, God was grieved and determined a new plan of direction. God had reluctantly given Saul to be king over His people in response to their demands (1 Sam. 8:6-7; see also 1 Sam. 15:10,11,23,35).

9. God changed His mind and decided to add fifteen years to King Hezekiah's reign. This was in response to humble prayer (2 Kings 20:1-7).

10. God gave David three options of punishment for sin. David chose the direct hand of God, banking upon the mercy of God. God did choose to extend mercy and stayed the angel's hand from further judgment (1 Chron. 21:11-15).

11. When King Rehoboam and his leaders humbled themselves, God changed His threatened judgment and granted them "some deliverance" (2 Chron. 12:5-8).

12. God declared that He will change His purpose of judgment and blessing in accordance with man's reactions (Jer. 18:5-10).

13. Jeremiah proclaimed the possibility of God changing His purpose of judgment if Israel would respond in repentance (Jer. 26:2-7,12-13).

14. God might be induced to change His judgment if Israel would turn to God with sincere repentance (Joel 2:12-14).

15. God's judgment upon Nineveh was averted by one of the greatest examples of mass repentance ever recorded (Jonah 3).

16. Names can be blotted out of the Book of Life (Rev. 3:5).

9

Good Guys/Bad Guys

Luke Skywalker versus Darth Vader; Superman versus sinister Lex Luthor; the Lone Ranger versus outlaws; Snow White versus the witch envious of her beauty. Whether in fiction or real life the conflict is ever the same: good guys versus bad guys. The bad guys are almost always in the majority, while the good guys are seemingly the underdogs. At the movies, most of us cheer for the good guys to triumph and we are rarely disappointed. (These days, however, it's often hard to discern who really are the good guys.)

The next thirteen lists explore these two categories. As usual, the bad guys eclipse the good guys in number. But in the end, guess who wins?

63. Twenty Instances of Exile

1. God drove *Adam* and *Eve* out of the Garden of Eden (Gen. 3:24).
2. The Lord exiled *Cain* to the land of Nod (Gen. 4:13-16).
3. *Noah, Shem, Ham, Japheth*, and their wives were exiled from their homes forever by the flood (Gen. 7:23).
4. In obedience to God, *Abram* exiled himself and his family from their home in Ur (Gen. 12:1-5).
5. Abraham banished *Hagar* and *Ishmael* (Gen. 21:14).
6. *Jacob* chose exile rather than constant contention with Esau (Gen. 27:41-45).
7. "*Joseph* was brought down to Egypt; and Potiphar . . . bought him" (Gen. 39:1).

8. The *children of Israel* were exiles in Egypt for 430 years (Ex. 12:40).

9. "*Moses* fled from the face of Pharaoh, and dwelt in the land of Midian" (Ex. 2:15).

10. "The *children of Israel* walked forty years in the wilderness" (Josh. 5:6).

11. "*Jephthah* fled from his brethren and dwelt in the land of Tob" (Judges 11:3).

12. *David* lived in exile when he was fleeing from Saul (1 Sam. 27:1-7).

13. After he had had Amnon killed, "*Absalom* fled, and went to Talmai . . . and was there three years" (2 Sam. 13:37,38).

14. "Solomon sought therefore to kill Jeroboam. And *Jeroboam* arose, and fled into Egypt . . . until the death of Solomon" (1 Kings 11:40).

15. Assyria carried *Israel* into exile (2 Kings 17:6).

16. Nebuchadnezzar carried all in *Jerusalem* to Babylon (2 Kings 24:14,15).

17. The remnant of *Judah,* including *Jeremiah,* was exiled to Egypt (Jer. 43:5-7).

18. *Joseph* and *Mary* fled with *Jesus* into Egypt until Herod died (Matt. 2:13-15).

19. "There was a great persecution against *the church* which was at Jerusalem; and they were all scattered abroad throughout the regions of Judaea and Samaria" (Acts 8:1).

20. *John* was exiled to Patmos (Rev. 1:9).

64. Prisons and Prisoners

1. *Joseph* was thrown into prison, where he met *Pharaoh's butler and baker* (Gen. 39:20-40:3).

2. As governor of Egypt, Joseph put *his brothers* in prison for three days and left *Simeon* there until his brothers returned with Benjamin (Gen. 42:17-24).

3. Joshua had the *five Amorite kings* sealed inside a cave, and then posted a guard until he could return for them (Josh. 10:16-18).

4. The Philistines put out *Samson*'s eyes and made him grind in the prison (Judges 16:21).

5. Ahab threw the prophet *Micaiah* into prison because he did not like Micaiah's prophecy (1 Kings 22:26,27).

6. The king of Assyria bound *King Hoshea* of Israel in prison (2 Kings 17:4).

7. *Jehoiachin,* king of Judah, was imprisoned in Babylon (2 Kings 25:27,28).
8. King Asa threw *Hanani* into prison for delivering an unfavorable word from the Lord (2 Chron. 16:10).
9. The king had *Jeremiah* put into prison and finally into a miry dungeon (Jer. 32:2; 37:16; 38:6).
10. The king of Babylon put out the eyes of *Zedekiah* and bound him in chains (Jer. 52:11).
11. Herod put *John the Baptist* into prison for speaking against Herod's adulterous marriage (Matt. 14:3,4).
12. *Jesus* was taken prisoner (John 18:12) and the convict *Barabbas* was released in His place (Matt. 27:26).
13. *Peter* and *John* spent a night in prison for preaching (Acts 4:3).
14. *The apostles* were imprisoned, but the angel of the Lord led them out at night (Acts 5:17,19).
15. Herod put *Peter* into prison, but an angel released him (Acts 12:4,6).
16. *Paul* was imprisoned with *Silas* at Philippi (Acts 16:22-24) and alone in Jerusalem (Acts 22:24,25), in Caesarea (Acts 23:33-35), and in Rome (Acts 28:16).

65. Fourteen Great Escapes

1. *Lot* and his *two daughters* escaped the destruction of Sodom after being warned by two angels (Gen. 19:15-26).
2. The ten plagues allowed the *600,000 Israelite men* (plus women and children) to escape from Egypt (Ex. 12:37).
3. The *two spies* that went to Jericho escaped because Rahab hid them on her roof, sent their pursuers off on a wild-goose chase, and let the spies down the wall with a rope that hung from her window (Josh. 2:1-22).
4. *Samson* escaped the Philistines by breaking new ropes that bound him. He then found the jawbone of an ass and killed 1,000 men before running away (Judges 15:11-15).
5. *Samson* escaped again by removing the doors from the gates of the city of Gaza and carrying them to the top of a nearby hill (Judges 16:1-3).
6. While *David* was fleeing from Saul, his wife let him down through a window and put an idol in his bed to fool Saul's messengers (1 Sam. 19:12-16).
7. *David* escaped the king of Gath by pretending to be a madman (1 Sam. 21:10-22:1).

8. *Jonathan* and *Ahimaaz* escaped from Absalom's men by hiding in a well that a woman covered to look like a pile of grain (2 Sam. 17:15-21).

9. *Jonah* tried to "flee unto Tarshish from the presence of the Lord." It didn't work (Jonah 1:3).

10. The people of the synagogue in Nazareth were going to

Paul escapes from Damascus

stone *Jesus,* "but he passing through the midst of them went his way" (Luke 4:29,30).

11. "[The Jews] sought again to take [*Jesus*]: but he escaped out of their hand" (John 10:39).
12. *The apostles,* and later *Peter* alone, were released from prison by angels (Acts 5:18,19; 12:6-10).
13. *Paul* escaped Jewish assassins in Damascus by leaving the city in a basket let down the side of the wall through a window (Acts 9:23-25).
14. *Paul* and *Silas* were released from prison in Philippi by an earthquake and then led out by the jailor (Acts 16:25-30).

66. Arsonists

1. *The children of Israel* burned the cities of Jericho (Josh. 6:24), Ai (Josh. 8:19), Hazor (Josh. 11:11), and all the cities of the Midianites (Num. 31:9,10).
2. *Israel* stoned Achan and then burned him and all his belongings (Josh. 7:24,25).
3. *Judah* fought the Canaanites at Jerusalem and burned the city (Judges 1:8).
4. *Abimelech and his men* burned down the tower of Shechem, killing about a thousand men and women (Judges 9:49).
5. *Samson* tied torches to foxes' tails and "let them go into the standing [grain] of the Philistines and burnt up both the shocks and also the standing [grain]" (Judges 15:4,5).
6. *Men of Dan* burned down the Canaanite city of Laish (Judges 18:26,27).
7. "*The men of Israel* turned again upon the children of Benjamin, and smote them with the edge of the sword. . . . Also they set on fire all the cities that they came to" (Judges 20:48).
8. *The Amalekites* burned David's city of Ziklag (1 Sam. 30:1).
9. *Absalom* burned Joab's barley field just to get his attention (2 Sam. 14:28-33).
10. "*Pharaoh* king of Egypt had gone up, and taken Gezer, and burnt it with fire" (1 Kings 9:16).
11. *King Zimri* committed suicide by burning down his house while he was in it (1 Kings 16:18).
12. *Nebuchadnezzar* burned Jerusalem (2 Kings 25:9).
13. *Ephesian converts* burned magic books worth 50,000 pieces of silver (Acts 19:19).

67. Thieves and Robbers

1. *"Rachel* had stolen the images that were her father's" (Gen. 31:19).
2. *Achan* took a beautiful Babylonian garment, a bar of silver, and a bar of gold during the battle at Ai (Josh. 7:11-21).
3. "The *men of Shechem* set liers in wait for Abimelech in the top of the mountains, and they robbed all that came along that way by them" (Judges 9:25).
4. *Micah* stole 1,100 shekels of silver from his mother (Judges 17:2).
5. Six hundred *Danites* stopped at Micah's house and stole his carved image, ephod, teraphim, and molten image (Judges 18:16-18).
6. The *people of Judah* were robbing the Lord of His rightful tithes (Mal. 3:8).
7. "Then were there *two thieves* crucified with Jesus, one on the right hand, and another on the left" (Matt. 27:38).
8. *Judas Iscariot* stole from the disciples' treasury (John 12:4-6).
9. "Now *Barabbas* was a robber" (John 18:40).

68. Impersonators

1. *Sarai* posed as Abram's sister in Egypt (Gen. 12:10-20).
2. *Rebekah* posed as Isaac's sister in Gerar (Gen. 26:6-11).
3. *Jacob* disguised himself as Esau so well that his father Isaac believed it (Gen. 27:1-29).
4. *Leah* posed as her sister Rachel when Jacob married her (Gen. 29:21-25).
5. *The Gibeonites* fooled Joshua by impersonating ambassadors from a distant country (Josh. 9:4-16).
6. *David* escaped from King Achish by pretending to be a madman (1 Sam. 21:12-22:1).
7. "*Saul* disguised himself, and put on other raiment, and he went" out to see the medium at Endor (1 Sam. 28:8).
8. Joab convinced *the wise woman of Tekoah* to pretend to be a mourning widow and to ask for King David's help (2 Sam. 14:1-24).
9. *Jeroboam's wife* disguised herself and went to the prophet Ahijah to find out what the future held, but the Lord told him who she was (1 Kings 14:1-6).

10. *A prophet* disguised himself as a wounded soldier in order to get a point across to King Ahab (1 Kings 20:35-43).
11. *King Ahab* disguised himself when fighting the Syrians, but a fatal arrow found him anyway (1 Kings 22:30-40).
12. *King Josiah* also disguised himself for battle against King Necho of Egypt. He too was fatally wounded (2 Chron. 35:20-24).
13. The chief priests and scribes sent *spies,* pretending to be sincere followers, to Jesus to try to trap him (Luke 20:19,20).

69. Four Kidnappers

1. Joseph was kidnapped and sold into slavery by *his brothers* (Gen. 37:17-28).
2. *The men of Benjamin* grabbed wives for themselves from the women of Shiloh during a festal dance (Judges 21:16-23).
3. Solomon had to judge a case in which two harlots had borne boys. One baby had died, and his *mother* had secretly traded the corpse for the other mother's son (1 Kings 3:16-21).
4. Prince Joash was kidnapped by his aunt *Jehosheba* to protect him from his murderous grandmother Athaliah (2 Kings 11:1-3).

70. Seven Good Kings—All from Judah

1. *David* was "a man after [God's] own heart" (1 Sam 13:14; Acts 13:22).
2. *Asa's* "heart was perfect with the Lord all his days" (1 Kings 15:11,14).
3. *Jehoshaphat* "turned not aside from ... doing what was right in the eyes of the Lord" (1 Kings 22:42,43).
4. *Uzziah* (also known as Azariah) "did that which was right in the eyes of the Lord" (2 Kings 15:1-3).
5. *Jotham* "did that which was right in the sight of the Lord" (2 Kings 15:32-34).
6. *Hezekiah* "did that which was right in the sight of the Lord" (2 Kings 18:1-3).
7. *Josiah* was like no other king in turning "to the Lord with all his heart, and with all his soul, and with all his might" (2 Kings 22:1,2; 23:25).

71. Thirty Bad Kings

1. *Jeroboam* the son of Nebat made two golden calves and appointed priests for the high places (1 Kings 12:28; 13:33,34).
2. *Rehoboam* (Judah) "did evil, because he prepared not his heart to seek the Lord" (2 Chron. 12:14).
3. *Abijam* (Judah) "walked in all the sins of his father" (1 Kings 15:1-3).
4. *Nadab* "made Israel to sin" (1 Kings 15:25,26).
5. *Baasha* "walked in the way of Jeroboam" (1 Kings 15:33,34).
6. *Elah* provoked the Lord to anger with his idols (1 Kings 16:8-14).
7. *Zimri* killed Elah to obtain the throne for a seven-day reign (1 Kings 16:9-20).
8. *Omri* "did worse than all that were before him" (1 Kings 16:25).
9. *Ahab* "did sell himself to work wickedness" like none other before him (1 Kings 16:30; 21:25).
10. *Ahaziah* son of Ahab "served Baal, and worshipped him" (1 Kings 22:51-53).
11. *Jehoram* son of Ahab "cleaved unto the sins of Jeroboam" (2 Kings 3:1-3).
12. *Jehoram* (Judah) son of Jehoshaphat "walked in the way of the kings of Israel" (2 Kings 8:16-18).
13. *Ahaziah* (Judah) son of Jehoram "did evil in the sight of the Lord" (2 Kings 8:25-27).
14. "*Jehu* took no heed to walk in the law of the Lord God of Israel" (2 Kings 10:29-31).
15. *Jehoahaz* the son of Jehu "followed the sins of Jeroboam" (2 Kings 13:1,2).
16. *Jehoash* the son of Jehoahaz "did that which was evil in the sight of the Lord" (2 Kings 13:10,11).
17. *Jeroboam* the son of Joash "did that which was evil in the sight of the Lord" (2 Kings 14:23,24).
18. *Zachariah* did "as his fathers had done" (2 Kings 15:8,9).
19. *Shallum* slew Zachariah to gain his throne (2 Kings 15:10).
20. *Menahem* "departed not all his days from the sins of Jeroboam" (2 Kings 15:17,18).
21. *Pekahiah* "did that which was evil in the sight of the Lord" (2 Kings 15:23,24).
22. *Pekah* killed Pekahiah to gain the throne (2 Kings 15:27,28).
23. *Ahaz* (Judah) sacrificed his son to idols (2 Kings 16:2-4).

24. *Hoshea* did evil and was finally carried away to exile in Assyria (Kings 17:1,2).
25. *Manasseh* (Judah) "built up again the high places which Hezekiah his father had destroyed" (2 Kings 21:1-7).
26. *Amon* (Judah) "forsook the Lord God of his fathers" (2 Kings 21:19-22).
27. *Jehoahaz* (Judah) the son of Josiah "did that which was evil in the sight of the Lord" (2 Kings 23:31,32).
28. *Jehoiakim* (Judah) did "according to all that his fathers had done" (2 Kings 23:36,37).
29. *Jehoiachin* (Judah) "did that which was evil in the sight of the Lord" (2 Kings 24:8,9).
30. *Zedekiah* (Judah) "did that which was evil in the sight of the Lord" (2 Kings 24:18,19).

72. Four Good Kings Who Became Bad

1. *Saul* was given a new heart by God, but he chose to disobey God continually (1 Sam. 10:9; 13:13,14).
2. *Solomon* loved the Lord, but in his old age, he was turned to evil by his heathen wives (1 Kings 3:3; 11:4).
3. *Jehoash* (also known as Joash) the son of Ahaziah "did that which was right in the sight of the Lord," but he later forsook the Lord (2 Kings 12:1,2; 2 Chron. 24:20-22).
4. *Amaziah* "did that which was right in the sight of the Lord," but he later turned away from following the Lord (2 Kings 14:1-3; 2 Chron. 25:1,2,27).

73. Four Adulterers

1. "*Reuben* went and lay with Bilhah his father's concubine" (Gen. 35:22).
2. *David* lay with Uriah's wife Bathsheba (2 Sam. 11:3,4).
3. "*Absalom* went in unto his father's concubines in the sight of all Israel" (2 Sam. 16:22).
4. The scribes and Pharisees caught *a woman* committing adultery and brought her to Jesus (John 8:3).

74. Four Swindlers

1. *Jacob* cheated Esau out of his birthright and his blessing (Gen. 27:36).

2. *Laban* cheated Jacob by giving him Leah instead of Rachel. He also changed Jacob's wages ten times (Gen. 29:21-25; 31:7).

3. The *Gibeonites* swindled a treaty from Joshua by telling him lies (Josh. 9:4-16).

4. *Ziba* tried to swindle his master Miphibosheth by lying to David (2 Sam. 16:1-4; 19:24-30).

75. Eighteen Traitors

1. *Absalom* conspired with Ahithophel to take over the kingdom of David (2 Sam. 15:31).

2. *Sheba* conspired against David, and all the men of Israel except the tribe of Judah followed Sheba (2 Sam. 20:1,2).

3. *Baasha* conspired against King Nadab and killed him (1 Kings 15:27).

4. King Elah's servant *Zimri,* who was captain of half his chariots, conspired against him and killed him (1 Kings 16:8-10).

5. *Hazael* murdered King Ben-hadad and reigned in his stead (2 Kings 8:7-15).

6. *Jehu* conspired against King Joram and killed him and all of the house of Ahab; and Jehu reigned over Israel (2 Kings 9:14-10:36).

7. "When *Athaliah* the mother of Ahaziah saw that her son was dead, she arose and destroyed all the seed royal . . . and Athaliah did reign over the land" (2 Kings 11:1,3).

8. Queen Athaliah accused *Jehoiada* the priest of treason for restoring the throne to Joash, the rightful ruler of Judah (2 Kings 11:14-16).

9. *Jozachar* and *Jehozabad* conspired against their master, King Joash, and slew him (2 Kings 12:20,21).

10. The *people of Jerusalem* conspired against King Amaziah, "and he fled to Lachish; but they sent after him to Lachish, and slew him there" (2 Kings 14:17-19).

11. "*Shallum* the son of Jabesh conspired against [King Zachariah], and smote him before the people, and slew him, and reigned in his stead" (2 Kings 15:10).

12. "*Menahem* the son of Gadi went up from Tirzah, and came to Samaria, and smote Shallum the son of Jabesh in Samaria, and slew him, and reigned in his stead" (2 Kings 15:14).

13. *Pekah* the son of Remaliah, a captain of [King Pekahiah],

90

Judas betrays Jesus with a kiss

conspired against him, and smote him in Samaria, in the
palace of the king's house" (2 Kings 15:25).

14. "*Hoshea* the son of Elah made conspiracy against Pekah
the son of Remaliah, and smote him, and slew him, and
reigned in his stead" (2 Kings 15:30).

15. "The king of Assyria found conspiracy in *Hoshea*: for he had sent messengers to So king of Egypt, and brought no present to the king of Assyria" (2 Kings 17:4).

16. *Adrammelech* and *Sharezer*, sons of King Sennacherib of Assyria, killed him while he worshiped his god Nisroch (2 Kings 19:37).

17. "The *servants of Amon* conspired against him, and slew the king in his own house" (2 Kings 21:23).

18. *Judas Iscariot* was the traitor who betrayed Jesus (Luke 6:16; 22:48).

10

The Spirit World

Many people deny that there is anything but a material world. Some acknowledge that there is a spiritual world, but that it consists of only good powers. Others say there are good powers and evil powers—some of these people would have you believe there is an evil power behind every problem and object in life. Still others claim that they not only believe in evil powers, but that they make contact with these powers and can exercise evil power any time they desire.

The rebirth of the popularity of occult practices in recent years can hardly escape our notice. A few years ago, a major section of an issue of *Time* magazine focused on the renaissance of the occult. In recent years an east coast university has been offering a degree in parapsychology—the study of occult phenomenon. The recent involvement of Kathryn Kübler Ross in several facets of the occult is a striking example of the direction many are taking today.

The Bible is not a textbook on occult phenomenon. However, it does mention many activities of spirit beings, including angels, demons, and Satan. The following nine lists show us what to watch out for as we face this growing movement.

76. Names of Angels in the Bible

1. When the angel of the Lord met with Manoah and his wife, he told them that his name was a secret (Judges 13:17,18).
2. Gabriel spoke with Daniel, Zacharias, and Mary (Dan. 8:15-17; Luke 1:19, 26,27).
3. Jude 9 tells about Michael the archangel.

77. Eleven Titles and Categories of Angels

1. Angel of light (2 Cor. 11:14).
2. Angel of the Lord (Gen. 16:7).
3. Angels of the churches (Rev. 1:20).
4. Archangel (Jude 9).
5. Cherubim (Gen. 3:24).
6. Chief prince (Dan. 10:13).
7. Devil's angels (Matt. 25:41).
8. Evil angels (Ps. 78:49).
9. "Guardian angels" (Matt. 18:10).
10. Seraphim (Isa. 6:1-6).
11. Watchers (Dan. 4:13,17,23).

78. Ten Statements by Satan and Demons

1. In opposition to God, Satan told Eve that she would not die for eating of the tree of the knowledge of good and evil. He said that Adam and Eve would "be as gods, knowing good and evil" (Gen. 3:1-5).
2. A spirit told God that he would be a lying spirit in the mouths of Ahab's prophets, thus bringing about Ahab's death on the battlefield (1 Kings 22:19-22).
3. Satan told the Lord that Job would curse God if everything Job had was taken away (Job 1:9-11).
4. After Job passed the first test, Satan told God that Job would curse the Lord if his body was afflicted (Job 2:1-5).
5. Lucifer's aspirations to be "like the most High" are recorded in Isa. 14:13,14.
6. The devil spoke to Jesus in the wilderness and tempted Him by quoting scripture out of context (Matt. 4:1-11).
7. When Jesus confronted demons who were inhabiting people, they acknowledged that Jesus was "the Holy One of God" (Luke 4:34) and "the Son of God" (Luke 4:41).
8. When Jesus confronted the Gadarene demoniac, the demons begged not to be tormented or sent into the deep. They identified themselves as "Legion" and asked to be sent into a herd of swine (Luke 8:26-32).
9. A demon-possessed soothsayer followed Paul and his companions, shouting that they were servants of God proclaiming the way of salvation (Acts 16:16-18).
10. When the seven sons of Sceva attempted to cast out an evil

94

The Gadarene demoniac

spirit, it answered them, "Jesus I know, and Paul I know; but who are ye?" (Acts 19:13-15).

79. Forty-three Past Activities of Angels

1. Cherubim guarded the tree of life in the Garden of Eden (Gen. 3:24).
2. The angel of the Lord found Hagar in the wilderness, prophesied to her, and sent her home (Gen. 16:7-12).

3. Two angels ate with Lot, blinded the Sodomites, and brought Lot and his family out of Sodom (Gen. 19:1-22).

4. The angel of God spoke to Hagar out of heaven and encouraged her (Gen. 21:17,18).

5. The angel of the Lord called to Abraham from heaven, stopped him from sacrificing Isaac, and told him that God would multiply his descendants (Gen. 22:11-18).

6. The angel of God spoke to Jacob in a dream and showed him how to get Laban's cattle (Gen. 31:11,12).

7. The angel of the Lord appeared to Moses in the burning bush and told him to go to Pharaoh and to bring the children of Israel out of Egypt (Ex. 3:1-22; 4:1-17).

8. The angel of God provided the pillar of fire and the pillar of cloud which went with the children of Israel as they traveled toward the Promised Land (Ex. 14:19,20).

9. The angel of the Lord withstood Balaam and his ass—first in a invisible form and then in a visible form. The angel warned Balaam to follow his orders (Num. 22:21-35).

10. The captain of the Lord's host appeared unto Joshua before the battle of Jericho (Josh. 5:13-15).

11. The angel of the Lord rebuked the children of Israel because they didn't stay separated from the people around them (Judges 2:1-4).

12. The angel of the Lord appeared to Gideon and told him that he was to deliver Israel from the Midianites (Judges 6:11-21).

13. The angel of the Lord appeared to Samson's parents and told them of Samson's impending birth (Judges 13:2-20).

14. An angel smote Israel with a pestilence that killed 70,000 men because David had taken a census (2 Sam. 24:15,16).

15. The angel of the Lord fed Elijah two meals (1 Kings 19:5-8).

16. The angel of the Lord gave Elijah a message for Israel's King Ahaziah, condemning his idolatry and foretelling his death (2 Kings 1:3,4).

17. "The angel of the Lord went out, and smote in the camp of the Assyrians an hundred fourscore and five thousand: and when they arose early in the morning, behold, they were all dead corpses" (2 Kings 19:35).

18. Isaiah saw and heard the seraphim praise and worship God (Isa. 6:1-3).

19. A seraph touched Isaiah's lips with a live coal and declared God's forgiveness to him (Isa. 6:5-7).

20. Nebuchadnezzar attributed the preservation of Shadrach, Meshech, and Abednego in the fiery furnace to God's angel (Dan. 3:28).

21. Daniel said, "My God hath sent his angel, and hath shut the lions' mouths, that they have not hurt me" (Dan. 6:22).

22. Twice Gabriel came to Daniel to give him understanding of future events (Dan. 8:15-26; 9:21-27).

23. Dan. 10:13-20 may refer to battles between good and evil angels.

24. The angel of the Lord prophesied and explained visions to Zechariah (Zech. 1:9-21; 2:3-5; 4:1-6).

25. The angel of the Lord appeared unto Joseph in a dream, told him that the Virgin Mary's pregnancy was of the Holy Spirit, and told him not to fear taking Mary to be his wife (Matt. 1:20).

26. The angel of the Lord again appeared to Joseph in a dream and told him to flee with Mary and Jesus to Egypt (Matt. 2:13).

27. After Herod had died, an angel again appeared to Joseph in a dream and told him that it was safe to return to Israel (Matt. 2:19,20).

28. Angels ministered to Jesus after His temptation by the devil (Matt. 4:11).

29. The angel of the Lord opened Jesus' tomb and gave the news of His resurrection to Mary Magdalene and the other Mary (Matt. 28:1-7).

30. The angel Gabriel foretold the birth of John the Baptist to his father-to-be, Zacharias (Luke 1:11-19).

31. Gabriel also announced to Mary that she would have a son, but that it would be a supernatural conception (Luke 1:26-38).

32. The angel of the Lord announced the birth of Jesus to the shepherds (Luke 2:8-14).

33. An angel told Mary to name her baby Jesus (Luke 2:21).

34. "The beggar [Lazarus] died, and was carried by the angels into Abraham's bosom" (Luke 16:22).

35. An angel from heaven appeared to Jesus in the garden of Gethsemane and strengthened him (Luke 22:43).

36. An angel of the Lord effected the apostles' escape from a Jerusalem prison. He told them to go and preach in the temple (Acts 5:19-20).

37. An angel told Philip to go south to a certain road. Philip met the Ethiopian eunuch along that road (Acts 8:26).

The angel Gabriel appears to Zacharias

38. An angel of God appeared to Cornelius in a vision and told him to send for the apostle Peter (Acts 10:3-6).
39. An angel woke Peter and freed him from prison in Jerusalem (Acts 12:6-10).
40. Because Herod did not give glory to God, an angel smote him (Acts 12:23).
41. As Paul was caught in a storm at sea, an angel assured him that all on board would live and that Paul would be brought before Caesar (Acts 27:23,24).
42. All the angels of God worshiped Jesus (Heb. 1:6).
43. Angels watched over churches (Rev. 1:20).

80. Eight Present Activities of Angels

1. "The angel of the Lord encampeth round about them that fear him, and delivereth them" (Ps. 34:7).
2. "He shall give his angels charge over thee, to keep thee in all thy ways. They shall bear thee up in their hands, lest thou dash thy foot against a stone" (Ps. 91:11,12).
3. It seems that children have "guardian angels" (Matt. 18:10).

4. "There is joy in the presence of the angels of God over one sinner that repenteth" (Luke 15:10).
5. Angels are "ministering spirits, sent forth to minister for them who shall be heirs of salvation" (Heb. 1:14).
6. Angels desire to look into the things of salvation (1 Pet. 1:12).
7. Angels watch over the churches (Rev. 1:20).
8. "I Jesus have sent mine angel to testify unto you these things in the churches" (Rev. 22:16).

81. Thirteen Future Activities of Angels

1. "In the end of this world, the Son of man shall send forth his angels, and they shall gather out of his kingdom all things that offend" (Matt. 13:40,41).
2. "The Son of man shall come in the glory of his Father with his angels; and then he shall reward every man according to his works" (Matt. 16:27).
3. The Son of man "shall send his angels with a great sound of a trumpet, and they shall gather together his elect from the four winds, from one end of heaven to the other" (Matt. 24:30,31).
4. Jesus said, "Hereafter ye shall see heaven open, and the angels of God ascending and descending upon the Son of man" (John 1:51).
5. Evil angels will be judged (2 Pet. 2:4).
6. Angels will watch over the churches (Rev. 1:20).
7. John "saw four angels standing on the four corners of the earth, holding the four winds of the earth, that the wind should not blow on the earth" (Rev. 7:1).
8. An angel will offer the prayers of the saints on the altar before God's throne (Rev. 8:3-5).
9. The angels will sound the seven trumpets of judgment (Rev. 8:7-10:7).
10. Michael and his angels will fight against the dragon and his angels (Rev. 12:7-10).
11. Seven angels will pour out vials of judgment upon the earth (Rev. 16:1-21).
12. An angel will cast Satan into the bottomless pit and bind him there (Rev. 20:1-3).
13. There will be an angel at each of the twelve gates of the New Jerusalem (Rev. 21:12).

82. Twenty-seven Past Activities of Satan and Demons

1. The serpent beguiled Eve and she ate of the forbidden fruit (Gen. 3:13).
2. Mediums were put to death in the Old Testament for dealing with familiar spirits (Lev. 20:27).
3. "God sent an evil spirit between Abimelech and the men of Shechem; and the men of Shechem dealt treacherously with Abimelech" (Judges 9:23).
4. An evil spirit bothered Saul and prophesied through him (1 Sam. 16:14-23; 18:10,11).
5. A lying spirit working through false prophets convinced Ahab to go into battle (1 Kings 22:20-22).
6. "Satan stood up against Israel, and provoked David to number Israel" (1 Chron. 21:1).
7. Satan took away Job's wealth, children, and health (Job 1:6-2:8).
8. Lucifer fell from heaven and weakened nations in his ambition to be like the Most High (Isa. 14:12-14).
9. "The Lord hath mingled a perverse spirit in the midst thereof: and they have caused Egypt to err in every work thereof" (Isa. 19:14).
10. The prince of the kingdom of Persia withstood an angel and kept him from going to Daniel for 21 days (Dan. 10:13).
11. Satan tempted Jesus (Matt. 4:1-11).
12. "They brought unto [Jesus] one possessed with a devil, blind, and dumb: and he healed him, insomuch that the blind and dumb both spake and saw" (Matt. 12:22).
13. A demon often sought to kill the boy it inhabited by casting him into fire or water. It would also throw him to the ground and cause him to grind his teeth and foam at the mouth (Mark 9:17-29).
14. An unclean spirit which recognized Jesus convulsed his victim before being cast out of him by Jesus (Mark 1:23-36).
15. "Legion" gave his victim insanity, great strength, and an inclination to harm himself (Mark 5:1-20).
16. Satan kept a woman bound for eighteen years by a spirit of infirmity so that she could not straighten herself (Luke 13:11-16).
17. Satan entered "into Judas surnamed Iscariot, . . . and

[Judas] went his way, and communed with the chief priests and captains, how he might betray [Jesus] unto them" (Luke 22:3,4).

18. Jesus said to Peter, "Simon, Simon, behold, Satan hath desired to have you, that he may sift you as wheat" (Luke 22:31).

19. The devil "was a murderer from the beginning, and abode not in the truth, because there is no truth in him. When he speaketh a lie, he speaketh of his own: for he is a liar, and the father of it" (John 8:44).

20. "Satan filled [Ananias'] heart to lie to the Holy Ghost, and to keep back part of the price of the land" (Acts 5:3).

21. "A certain damsel possessed with a spirit of divination . . . brought her masters much gain by soothsaying" (Acts 16:16).

22. The seven sons of Sceva were overcome by an evil spirit that they were trying to cast out of a man (Acts 19:16).

23. Satan hindered Paul from going to the Thessalonians (1 Thess. 2:18).

24. The devil has taken people captive at his will (2 Tim. 2:26).

25. The devil had the power of death (Heb. 2:14).

26. "The devil sinneth from the beginning" (1 John 3:8).

27. The devil disputed with Michael the archangel about the body of Moses (Jude 9).

83. Seven Present Activities of Satan and Demons

1. Demons may leave and later return to a person (Matt. 12:43-45).

2. Satan may take away the word that has been sown in people's hearts if they don't understand it (Matt. 13:19).

3. "The god of this world hath blinded the minds of them which believe not, lest the light of the glorious gospel of Christ, who is the image of God, should shine unto them" (2 Cor. 4:4).

4. Satan disguises himself as an angel of light (2 Cor. 11:14).

5. The powers of darkness fight against the saints (Eph. 6:12).

6. The devils believe in God and tremble (James 2:19).

7. The devil accuses us before our God day and night (Rev. 12:10).

84. Six Future Activities of Satan and Demons

1. Lucifer shall "be brought down to hell, to the sides of the pit" (Isa. 14:15).
2. "In the latter times some shall depart from the faith, giving heed to seducing spirits, and doctrines of devils" (1 Tim. 4:1).
3. Satan and his angels will battle Michael and his angels. Satan and his angels will be defeated and cast out of heaven to the earth (Rev. 12:7-10).
4. Spirits of devils will perform miracles to bring the nations to war (Rev. 16:13,14).
5. Satan will be cast into the bottomless pit for 1,000 years (Rev. 20:1-3).
6. Satan will be released upon the earth after the 1,000 years, but he will finally be cast into the lake of fire (Rev. 20:7-10).

11

Heathen Practices

Most people, when first confronting the scene of fifteen or twenty devout Hare Krishna members in a local park, bowing before a picture of an Indian deity, are awestruck. To think that such a practice could take place in our American communities is shocking to most of us. It's heathen; it's something foreign; it's strange and we don't like it. Even though we may not like it, there is little in the legal realm we can do about it.

The Bible records many pagan deities and practices that God had forbidden Israel to involve itself with. These pagan gods were an abomination to Him, and the practices associated with them were heinous. Worship of some of these gods went so far as human sacrifice. Recorded in the next lists are names of these gods, practicing sorcerers and witches, and different sacrifices made to those idols.

A pagan deity is, according to Arthur Wallis, "any person or thing that has usurped in the heart the place of preeminence that belongs to Jesus Christ." Though few around us bow with shaven head to an Eastern deity, many bow before Western values of prosperity, success, and prominence. Such "gods" may not look so strange, but the effect of worshiping them will be the same as that of worshiping idols.

85. Thirty-one Pagan Gods in the Bible

1. The Sepharites burned their children to *Adrammelech* (2 Kings 17:31).
2. The Sepharites also worshiped *Anammelech* (2 Kings 17:31).
3. The men of Hamath made *Ashima* (2 Kings 17:30).

4. Solomon worshiped *Ashtoreth* the goddess of the Zidonians (1 Kings 11:5) also known as the *queen of heaven* (Jer. 44:17).

5. King Ahab and Queen Jezebel served *Baal* (1 Kings 16:31,32).

6. After Gideon died, Israel turned to *Baal-berith* (Judges 8:33).

7. Israel served *Baal-peor*, the god of Moab (Num. 25:1-3).

8. *Baal-zebub* was the god of Ekron (2 Kings 1:2).

9. *Bel* was a Babylonian god (Jer. 51:44).

10. Aaron made the children of Israel a *molten calf* to worship (Ex. 32:1-5), and King Jeroboam made *golden calves* (1 Kings 12:26-30).

11. Castor was a Greek god (Acts 28:11).

12. Solomon built a high place for *Chemosh*, the abomination of Moab (1 Kings 11:7).

13. Amos chastised Israel for serving *Chiun* (Amos 5:26).

14. The Philistines had a temple for *Dagon* (1 Sam 5:1-5).

15. The great temple of the goddess *Diana* was in Ephesus (Acts 19:35).

16. The Lycaonians worshiped *Jupiter* (Acts 14:11-13).

17. The Roman god *Mercury* was also worshiped by the Lycaonians (Acts 14:11-13).

18. Solomon worshiped *Milcom*, the abomination of the Ammonites (1 Kings 11:5).

19. Solomon built a high place for *Molech*, the god of Ammon (1 Kings 11:7).

20. Isaiah said that the people served *Nebo* (Isa. 46:1).

21. Israel saved the brass serpent that Moses made and worshiped it. They called it *Nehushtan* (2 Kings 18:4).

22. The men of Cuth worshiped *Nergal* (2 Kings 17:30).

23. The Avites worshiped *Nibhaz* (2 Kings 17:31).

24. Sennacherib, king of Assyria, was killed while worshiping *Nisroch* (2 Kings 19:36,37).

25. *Pollux* was a Greek god (Acts 28:11).

26. Israel worshiped images of *Remphan* (Acts 7:43).

27. *Rimmon* was the god of the Syrians (2 Kings 5:17, 18).

28. The Babylonians worshiped *Succoth-benoth* (2 Kings 17:30).

29. Ezekiel saw a woman weeping for the god *Tammuz* (Ezek. 8:14).

30. The Avites worshiped *Tartak* (2 Kings 17:31).

31. Micah built a shrine for his *teraphim*, or household gods (Judges 17:5).

Sennacherib is murdered while worshiping Nisroch

86. Witches and Sorcerers

1. Pharaoh called on his *sorcerers* and *magicians* to duplicate the miracles that Moses performed (Ex. 7:11,12).
2. The witch of Endor was a *medium* (1 Sam. 28:7-25).
3. Jezebel practiced *witchcraft* (2 Kings 9:22).
4. Edom, Moab, Ammon, Tyre, and Aidon all had *enchanters, sorcerers,* and *diviners* (Jer. 27:3-10).
5. Nebuchadnezzar's *magicians, astrologers, soothsayers*, and *sorcerers* could neither tell him his dream nor interpret it (Dan. 2:10).
6. Nahum called Nineveh the mistress of *witchcrafts* (Nah. 3:4).
7. Simon amazed the people of Samaria with his *sorcery* (Acts 8:9).
8. Elymas was a *sorcerer* on the island of Paphos (Acts 13:6-8).
9. Many of those who repented and believed at Ephesus had practiced *curious arts* (Acts 19:19).

87. Sacrifices Made to Idols

1. The children of Israel "offered burnt offerings, and brought peace offerings" to the molten calf which Aaron made (Ex. 32:6).
2. Jeroboam offered sacrifices and burned incense to the two golden calves that he had made (1 Kings 12:32-33).
3. Elijah challenged the prophets of Baal to a contest in which they offered a bullock to their god (1 Kings 18:25).
4. The king of Moab despaired in the face of battle and offered his oldest son, the heir to the throne, as a burnt offering to his god (2 Kings 3:26,27).
5. "The Sepharvites burnt their children in fire to Adrammelech and Anammelech, the gods of Sepharvaim" (2 Kings 17:31).

Saul and the witch at Endor

6. The children of Israel burned incense to the brazen serpent which Moses had made (2 Kings 18:4).
7. Idolatrous priests burned incense to Baal (2 Kings 23:5).
8. The Israelites offered up their children in the fire of Molech (2 Kings 23:10).
9. Ahaz burned incense and offered his children to Molech. He also sacrificed and burned incense to Asherah and the gods of Damascus (2 Chron. 28:1-4,23).
10. The people of Judah burned incense, sacrificed cakes, and poured out drink offerings to the queen of heaven (Jer. 44:19).
11. The people of Jerusalem offered meat, fine flour, oil, honey, and even their sons and daughters to idols (Ezek. 16:17-20).

12

What's My Line?

A recent advertisement in major national magazines quoted Christopher Morley's maxim, "There is only one success . . . to be able to spend your life in your own way." In the background a man sat alone, fishing in a setting of idyllic beauty. The American dream has developed to the point where we are made to feel that the only satisfying thing in life is doing what *I* want whenever *I* want. Work is now viewed as a necessary evil, for sustaining the leisure that one finds satisfying. Work is seldom looked upon as a satisfying part of one's life.

The Bible lists that follow show many of the vocations of those who lived in Bible times. They may not have had computers and copying machines to speed up their work, but the vocations that most of them pursued are quite similar to the vocations that many of us have. Yet, we find little discontentment among them concerning their jobs—as if they sensed God's purpose for their life while working.

Dorothy L. Sayers said, "I ask that work should be looked upon, not as a necessary drudgery to be undergone for the purpose of making money, but as a way of life in which the nature of man should find its proper exercise and delight and so fulfill itself to the glory of God."

88. Spies

1. The Lord commanded Moses to send twelve men into Canaan to spy out the land (Num. 13:1-16).
2. "Joshua the son of Nun sent out of Shittim two men to spy secretly, saying, Go view the land, even Jericho" (Josh. 2:1).

3. Spies found the entrance to the Canaanite city of Bethel before the army of Ephraim came in to destroy it (Judges 1:23-25).

4. The Danites sent five men to spy out the rest of their inheritance (Judges 18:2-28).

5. David sent spies out to see if Saul had followed him to the Wilderness of Ziph. He had (1 Sam. 26:3,4).

6. "Absalom sent spies throughout all the tribes of Israel, saying, As soon as ye hear the sound of the trumpet, then ye shall say, Absalom reigneth in Hebron" (2 Sam. 15:10).

7. Hushai, the counselor of Absalom, was actually a spy for David (2 Sam. 15:32-37).

8. The chief priests and scribes sent spies to watch Jesus (Luke 20:20).

9. Paul wrote with concern about "false brethren unawares brought in, who came in privily to spy out our liberty which we have in Christ Jesus, that they might bring us into bondage" of the law (Gal. 2:4).

89. Godly Officials in Heathen Governments

1. Pharaoh appointed *Joseph* to be governor over Egypt (Gen. 41:39-41).

2. *Nehemiah* was Artaxerxes' cupbearer (Neh. 1:11-2:1).

3. *Esther* became queen to Ahasuerus (Esther 2:17).

4. "*Mordecai* the Jew was next unto King Ahasuerus, and great among the Jews" (Esther 10:3).

5. "King Nebuchadnezzar made *Daniel* a great man, and gave him many gifts, and made him ruler over the whole province of Babylon, and chief of the governors over all the wise men of Babylon" (Dan. 2:48).

6. *Shadrach, Meshach,* and *Abednego* were appointed administrators over the province of Babylon by King Nebuchadnezzar (Dan. 2:49).

7. A godly *Roman centurion* asked Jesus to heal his servant (Luke 7:2-10).

8. The *Ethiopian eunuch* was a man "of great authority under Candace queen of the Ethiopians, who had the charge of all her treasure, and had come to Jerusalem for to worship" (Acts 8:27).

9. *Cornelius,* a Roman centurion in Caesarea, was "a devout man, and one that feared God with all his house, which gave

Esther becomes queen

much alms to the people, and prayed to God alway" (Acts 10:1,2).
10. *Sergius Paulus,* the proconsul of Cyprus, became a believer (Acts 13:7-12).
11. Paul greeted the Philippian church from the saints "that are of *Caesar's household*" (Phil. 4:22).

90. Artists and Craftsmen

1. Jubal was the inventor of the harp and the pipe (Gen. 4:21).
2. Tubal-cain was "an instructor of every artificer in brass and iron" (Gen. 4:22).
3. Noah built the ark of gopher wood (Gen. 6:13-22).
4. Bezaleel worked in gold, silver, brass, stone, and wood (Ex. 31:1-6).

5. Aaron made a molten calf of gold and fashioned it with a graving tool (Ex. 32:4).
6. Moses hewed two tables of stone to replace the ones he broke (Ex. 34:1,4).
7. Aholiab was an engraver and an embroiderer (Ex. 38:23).
8. "Moses made a serpent of brass" (Num. 21:9).
9. Hiram was "cunning to work all works in brass" (1 Kings 7:13,14).
10. Harhaiah was a goldsmith (Neh. 3:8).
11. Joseph was a carpenter (Matt. 13:55).
12. Jesus was a carpenter (Mark 6:3).
13. Paul, Aquila, and Priscilla were tentmakers (Acts 18:1-3).
14. Demetrius was a silversmith in Ephesus (Acts 19:24).
15. Alexander was a coppersmith (2 Tim. 4:14).

91. Physicians

1. "Joseph commanded his servants the physicians to embalm his father: and the physicians embalmed Israel" (Gen. 50:2).
2. King Asa was diseased in his feet and he sought the physicians but not the Lord (2 Chron. 16:12,13).
3. Luke, the beloved physician, sent greetings to the saints at Colosse (Col. 4:14).

92. Teachers

1. The Lord taught Moses what to say and what to do (Ex. 4:12,15).
2. Moses taught the children of Israel "ordinances and laws, and . . . the way wherein they must walk, and the work that they must do" (Ex. 18:20).
3. The Lord appointed Bezaleel and Aholiab to teach those who would construct the tabernacle (Ex. 35:30-35).
4. The Lord told Aaron to "teach the children of Israel all the statutes which the Lord hath spoken unto them by the hand of Moses" (Lev. 10:11).
5. The priests were to teach the children of Israel how to recognize and to deal with leprosy (Deut. 24:8).
6. The king of Assyria sent one of the exiled priests back to Samaria to teach the Gentile inhabitants how they should fear God (2 Kings 17:28).
7. King Jehoshaphat sent his princes throughout Judah to teach the law of the Lord to all the people (2 Chron. 17:7-9).

8. King Artaxerxes commissioned Ezra to teach the laws of God to Israel (Ezra 7:25).
9. Jesus taught the people (Matt. 11:1).
10. Jesus told His apostles, "Go ye therefore, and teach all nations, . . . to observe all things whatsoever I have commanded you" (Matt. 28:19,20).
11. Jesus said, "The Comforter, . . . shall teach you all things, and bring all things to your remembrance" (John 14:26).
12. "Paul and Barnabas continued in Antioch, teaching and preaching the word of the Lord, with many others also" (Acts 15:35).
13. Apollos taught in the synagogue at Ephesus, but Aquilla and Priscilla instructed him in the ways of God (Acts 18:24-26).
14. Paul disputed daily in the school of Tyrannus (Acts 19:9).
15. Paul was "brought up . . . at the feet of Gamaliel, and taught according to the perfect manner of the law of the fathers" (Acts 22:3).

93. Shepherds

1. Abel was a keeper of sheep (Gen. 4:2).
2. Abram had sheep (Gen. 12:16).
3. Rachel was a shepherdess (Gen. 29:9).
4. Laban had sheep (Gen. 29:9).
5. Jacob had sheep (Gen. 32:14).
6. Jacob's sons tended his flocks (Gen. 37:13).
7. Judah had sheep (Gen. 38:12,13).
8. Moses' wife Zipporah and her sisters tended their father's sheep (Ex. 2:16,17).
9. Moses became a shepherd for his father-in-law's flock (Ex. 3:1).
10. Achan kept sheep (Josh. 7:24).
11. David was a shepherd (1 Sam. 16:11-13).
12. Nabal had three thousand sheep (1 Sam. 25:2,3).
13. Job had fourteen thousand sheep (Job 42:12).
14. David said, "The Lord is my shepherd" (Ps. 23:1).
15. Jesus said, "I am the good shepherd: the good shepherd giveth his life for the sheep" (John 10:11).
16. Jesus commanded Peter to shepherd the church (John 21:15-17).

112

94. *Beggars*

1. "Blind Bartimaeus, the son of Timaeus, sat by the highway side begging" (Mark 10:46).
2. Jesus spoke about a beggar named Lazarus who died and

Boaz sees Ruth gleaning in his field

was carried by the angels into Abraham's bosom (Luke 16:20-22).

3. Jesus healed a blind beggar by putting mud on his eyes and sending him to wash in the pool of Siloam (John 9:1-8).
4. Peter and John healed a lame beggar who had been asking for alms at the temple gate (Acts 3:2-7).

95. Thirteen Famous Farmers

1. "The Lord God planted a garden eastward in Eden" (Gen. 2:8).
2. "Cain was a tiller of the ground" (Gen. 4:2).
3. "Noah began to be an husbandman, and he planted a vineyard" (Gen. 9:20).
4. "Isaac sowed in [Gerar], and received in the same year an hundredfold" (Gen. 26:12).
5. Gideon raised wheat (Judges 6:11).
6. Boaz had a barley field (Ruth 1:22-2:3).
7. David commanded Ziba to till the land for Mephibosheth, Saul's grandson (2 Sam. 9:9,10).
8. Joab had a barley field (2 Sam. 14:30).
9. Elisha was plowing when Elijah threw his mantle upon him (1 Kings 19:19).
10. Naboth had a vineyard on which Ahab wanted to raise herbs (1 Kings 21:1,2).
11. King Uzziah loved husbandry (2 Chron. 26:9,10).
12. Job was a farmer (Job 1:14).
13. Solomon planted vineyards, gardens, and orchards (Eccles. 2:4, 5).

96. One Hundred and Ninety-eight Vocations in the Bible

1. Apostle (Acts 6:1-6).
2. Apothecary (perfumer) (Neh. 3:8).
3. Archer (Gen. 21:20).
4. Armorbearer (1 Sam. 14:12).
5. Astrologer (Dan. 1:20).
6. Baker (Gen. 40:1).
7. Barber (Ezek. 5:1).
8. Beggar (Acts 3:2).
9. Binder of sheaves (Ps. 129:7).

10. Bishop (or elder) (1 Tim. 3:1).
11. Brickmaker (Ex. 5:7).
12. Builder (1 Kings 5:18).
13. Butler (Gen. 40:1).
14. Calker (shipwright) (Ezek. 27:27).
15. Camel driver (Gen. 32:13-16; 33:13).
16. Candlestick maker (Ex. 25:31).
17. Carpenter (Mark 6:3).
18. Cattleman (Gen. 46:34).
19. Centurion (Matt. 8:5).
20. Chamberlain (Acts 12:20).
21. Chancellor (Ezra 4:8).
22. Chapman (trader) (2 Chron. 9:14).
23. Chariot driver (1 Kings 22:34).
24. Charmer (Ps. 58:5).
25. Clothes maker (Acts 9:39).
26. Confectionary (perfumer) (1 Sam. 8:13).
27. Cook (1 Sam. 8:13).
28. Coppersmith (2 Tim. 4:14).
29. Council (Sanhedrin) member (Acts 22:30).
30. Counsellor (1 Chron. 27:33).
31. Cupbearer (Neh. 1:11).
32. Daysman (mediator) (Job 9:33).
33. Deacon (Acts 6:3-5; 1 Tim. 3:8).
34. Deputy (governor) (Acts 13:7).
35. Ditchdigger (Isa. 22:11).
36. Diviner (1 Sam. 6:2).
37. Doorkeeper (1 Chron. 15:23).
38. Drawer of Water (Josh. 9:21).
39. Embroiderer (Ex. 38:23).
40. Enchanter (Jer. 27:9).
41. Engraver (Ex. 38:23).
42. Evangelist (Acts 21:8).
43. Exchanger (banker) (Matt. 25:27).
44. Executioner (Mark 6:27).
45. Exorcist (Acts 19:13).
46. Fanner (winnower) (Jer. 51:2).
47. Farmer (Matt. 22:5; Gen. 9:20 [husbandman]).
48. Feller (lumberjack) (Isa. 14:8).
49. Fisherman (Luke 5:2).
50. Footman (1 Sam. 22:17).
51. Forestkeeper (Neh. 2:8).

52. Fowler (Ps. 124:7).
53. Fruit gatherer (Amos 7:14).
54. Fuller (Mark 9:3).
55. Furniture maker (Ex. 31:6-9).
56. Gardener (John 20:15).
57. Garment maker (Ex. 31:6,10).
58. Goatherder (Gen. 32:14,16).
59. Goldsmith (Isa. 40:19).
60. Governor (Gen. 42:6).
61. Grapegatherer (Jer. 6:9).
62. Guard (Gen. 40:4).
63. Harlot (Josh. 6:17).
64. Harper (Rev. 14:2).
65. Herald (Dan. 3:4).
66. Hewer of timber (2 Chron. 2:10).
67. Hewer of wood (Josh. 9:21).
68. Horseman (2 Kings 9:17).
69. Hunter (Gen. 25:27).
70. Innkeeper (Luke 10:34,35).
71. Interpreter (Gen. 42:23).
72. Jailor (Acts 16:23).
73. Judge (2 Sam. 15:4).
74. King (Acts 25:13).
75. Lamp maker (Ex. 25:37).
76. Lawyer (Titus 3:13).
77. Lieutenant (Esther 9:3).
78. Locksmith (Neh. 3:3).
79. Magician (Dan. 2:2).
80. Magistrate (Acts 16:35).
81. Maid (Esther 4:4; Gen 16:1 [handmaid]).
82. Maidservant (Ex. 20:10).
83. Manservant (Ex. 20:10).
84. Mariner (Ezek. 27:27).
85. Mason (2 Kings 12:12).
86. Masterbuilder (1 Cor. 3:10).
87. Merchant (Rev. 18:11-13).
88. Messenger (1 Sam. 23:27).
89. Midwife (Gen. 35:17).
90. Miller (Matt. 24:41).
91. Miner (Job 28:1, 2).
92. Minister (Jer. 33:21).
93. Minstrel (2 Kings 3:15).

94. Moneychanger (Matt. 21:12).
95. Mourner (Eccles. 12:5).
96. Mover (Num. 4:1-15).
97. Musician (Ps. 4, title).
98. Necromancer (Deut. 18:11).
99. Night watchman (Isa. 21:11).
100. Nurse for children (Ex. 2:7-9).
101. Officer (Luke 12:58).
102. Orator (Acts 24:1).
103. Overseer (2 Chron. 34:12).
104. Pastor (Eph. 4:11).
105. Philosopher (Acts 17:18).
106. Physician (Col. 4:14).
107. Pilot (ship) (Ezek. 27:27).
108. Planter (Jer. 31:5).
109. Plowman (Amos 9:13).
110. Poet (Acts 17:28).
111. Porter (gatekeeper) (2 Kings 7:10).
112. Post (postman) (Esther 3:13).
113. Potter (Jer. 18:4).
114. Preacher (1 Tim. 2:7).
115. Presbyter (1 Tim. 4:14).
116. President (Dan. 6:2).
117. Priest (Hebrew) (Lev. 1:7).
118. Priest (pagan) (1 Sam. 6:2).
119. Prince (1 Chron. 5:6).
120. Prognosticator (Isa. 47:13).
121. Prophet (1 Sam. 3:20).
122. Prophetess (Judges 4:4).
123. Prostitute (see Harlot).
124. Publican (Luke 5:27).
125. Queen (1 Kings 10:1).
126. Rabbi (John 1:38).
127. Reaper (Amos 9:13; Isa. 17:5 [harvestman]).
128. Recorder (2 Sam. 8:16).
129. Refiner (Mal. 3:3).
130. Robber (Job 5:5).
131. Rower (Ezek. 27:26).
132. Runner (2 Sam. 15:1).
133. Sailor (Rev. 18:17).
134. Sawyers (2 Sam. 12:31).
135. Schoolmaster (Gal. 3:25).

136. Scientist (Dan. 1:4).
137. Scribe (2 Sam. 8:17).
138. Seamstress (Acts 9:39).
139. Seer (1 Sam. 9:9).
140. Seller (James 4:13).
141. Senator (Ps. 105:22).
142. Sergeant (Acts 16:35).
143. Servant (Gen. 24:2).
144. Sheepmaster (2 Kings 3:4).
145. Sheepshearer (Gen. 38:12).
146. Shepherd (Gen. 46:32; Amos 7:14 [herdman]).
147. Sheriff (Dan. 3:2).
148. Shipbuilder (1 Kings 22:48).
149. Shipmaster (Jonah 1:6).
150. Shipmen (1 Kings 9:27).
151. Silversmith (Acts 19:24; Judges 17:4 [founder]).
152. Singer (1 Chron. 9:33).
153. Slave (Rev. 18:13).
154. Slinger (2 Kings 3:25).
155. Smith (1 Sam. 13:19).
156. Snake charmer (Ps. 58:4, 5).
157. Soldier (Acts 27:31).
158. Soothsayer (Josh. 13:22).
159. Sorcerer (Ex. 7:11).
160. Sorceress (Isa. 57:3).
161. Sower (Isa. 55:10).
162. Spearman (Acts 23:23).
163. Spice merchant (1 Kings 10:15).
164. Spy (Josh. 2:1).
165. Stargazer (Isa. 47:13).
166. Steward (Gen. 15:2).
167. Stone cutter (1 Kings 5:18).
168. Swineherder (Mark 5:14).
169. Swordsman (Song of Sol. 3:8).
170. Tailor (Ex. 39:22).
171. Tanner (Acts 9:43).
172. Taskmaster (Ex. 1:11).
173. Tax collector (see Publican).
174. Teacher (1 Chron. 25:8).
175. Temple servants (Ezra 8:20).
176. Tentmaker (Acts 18:3).
177. Tetrarch (Matt. 14:1).

178. Thief (Joel 2:9).
179. Tormentor (Matt. 18:34).
180. Townclerk (Acts 19:35).
181. Treader of grapes (Amos 9:13).
182. Treasurer (Ezra 1:8).
183. Trumpeter (2 Kings 11:14).
184. Tutor (Gal. 4:2).
185. Usurer (Ex. 22:25).
186. Vinedresser (2 Kings 25:12).
187. Waiter (Acts 6:2).
188. Wardrobe keeper (2 Kings 22:14).
189. Watcher (Jer. 4:16).
190. Watchman (2 Kings 9:17).
191. Water drawer (Josh. 9:21).
192. Weapons maker (1 Sam. 8:12).
193. Weaver (Ex. 35:35).
194. Whore (Lev. 21:7).
195. Witch (Ex. 22:18).
196. Wizard (Lev. 20:27).
197. Woodcarver (Ex. 35:33).
198. Worker in brass (1 Kings 7:13, 14).

13

Money

"Federal Income Taxes Will Rise Thirteen Percent"—so reads the morning's headline. What's new? Year after year, it seems that government revenues fall short, so more is demanded. The IRS is busy making sure that we have paid all that is required of us. In hard economic times the burden of taxes becomes heavier and the percentage of poor people increases. Pressures to maintain our standard of living have even pushed many into illegal means of gaining money—extortion and bribery.

What is so true today was also true in the Bible times: taxes, government tax collectors, the poor becoming poorer, extortion, and bribery. Governments back then were well known to spend money lavishly on those in power and squeeze the little people for all they could get. Maybe we don't have it as bad as we think!

You may also want to reconsider the possible benefits of not being rich. The first lists show poor people and it is interesting how many of them received God's *direct* care because of their distressing situation. Had they not had such need, they might not have encountered God as they did. It's something to think about.

97. Poor People

1. Naomi and Ruth were poor when they came to the land of Israel from Moab (Ruth 1:21).
2. David was poor in his early days (1 Sam. 18:23).
3. A poor widow came to Elisha because a creditor wanted payment. It seems that the only assets she had to pay him with were a pot of oil and her two sons (2 Kings 4:1-2).
4. The widow of Zarephath was very poor and might have

starved to death if the Lord had not sent Elijah to her (1 Kings 17:8-16).

5. When the king of Babylon carried the people of Jerusalem away into captivity, he left only "the poorest sort of the people in the land" (2 Kings 24:10-14).

6. Blind Bartimaeus was a beggar before Jesus healed him (Mark 10:46).

7. Jesus commended a poor widow to His disciples, for putting all she had into the temple treasury (Mark 12:41-44).

8. When Lazarus the beggar died, angels carried him to Abraham's bosom (Luke 16:20-22).

9. Jesus healed another beggar who was blind from birth (John 9:1-8).

10. Peter and John healed a beggar lame from birth as they were going to the temple to pray (Acts 3:1-8).

11. Christians in Macedonia and Achaia made a contribution for the poor among the Jerusalem saints (Rom. 15:25-27).

The Macedonian believers contribute to the poor in Jerusalem

12. "Ye know the grace of our Lord Jesus Christ, that, though he was rich, yet for your sakes he became poor, that ye through his poverty might be rich" (2 Cor. 8:9).

98. Taxes

1. At Joseph's advice, the Egyptians were taxed 20 percent of their produce for the seven plenteous years before the famine. This tax remained even after the famine (Gen. 41:34; 47:26).
2. All Israelites twenty years old or older were required to pay a half shekel when the census was taken. The money was used for the service of the tabernacle (Ex. 30:12-16).
3. When Israel asked for a king, Samuel warned the people that he would tax them and take their children and property. Nevertheless, the people held to their request (1 Sam. 8).
4. Solomon's "heavy yoke" upon Israel probably included taxes (1 Kings 12:1-14).
5. The kingdoms Solomon reigned over brought "presents," or tribute, to his government (1 Kings 4:21).
6. Menahem, king of Israel, taxed the rich men of his kingdom fifty shekels of silver apiece to pay Pul, king of Assyria (2 Kings 15:19-20).
7. King Hoshea of Israel paid tribute to King Shalmaneser of Assyria. When it was discovered that he had ceased payments, Shalmaneser imprisoned him (2 Kings 17:3-4).
8. King Jehoiakim of Judah taxed his subjects in order to give Pharaoh Necho the tribute he demanded (2 Kings 23:33-35).
9. "Some of the Philistines brought Jehoshaphat [king of Judah] presents, and tribute silver" (2 Chron. 17:11).
10. The Jews were paying "toll, tribute, and custom" to Persia during Artaxerxes' reign (Ezra 4:13).
11. Later, King Artaxerxes exempted the priests, Levites, and other temple personnel from taxation (Ezra 7:24).
12. King Ahasuerus laid a tribute upon the land, and upon the isles of the sea [i.e., upon the whole empire]" (Esther 10:1).
13. Jesus sent Peter fishing to pay their taxes. In the fish's mouth was a coin sufficient for the tax (Matt. 17: 24-27).
14. Caesar imposed tribute on his subjects in Jerusalem in Jesus' day (Matt. 22:17-22).

122

15. Joseph and Mary had to go to Bethlehem to be registered before being taxed. Thus Jesus was born there (Luke 2:1-7).

99. Tax Collectors

1. Matthew (Levi) left his tax collecting to follow Jesus (Matt. 9:9).
2. Matthew then made a feast for Jesus, which many tax collectors (publicans) attended (Luke 5:29-32).
3. Zacchaeus, a rich chief tax collector, climbed a sycamore tree to see Jesus. When Jesus saw Zacchaeus and called him, he joyfully received Jesus into his home and was saved (Luke 19:1-10).
4. In one of Jesus' parables, a publican humbly prayed for mercy and was justified, whereas the self-exalting Pharisee was not (Luke 18:9-14).
5. Tax collectors came to John to be baptized; he charged them not to collect more than they were supposed to (Luke 3:12,13).

The widow's mite

100. Important Coins

1. The only coin mentioned in the Old Testament is the *dram* or *daric,* a gold Persian coin (Ezra 2:69; 8:27).
   Note: The coins mentioned in the New Testament were issued by three governments: Greek, Roman, and Jewish (Maccabaean). For the sake of clarity, it is necessary to refer to the names of the coins as given in the Greek text.
2. Sparrows were sold two for an *assarion* (farthing in KJV), a Greek coin (Matt. 10:29; cf. Luke 12:6).
3. The woman's lost coin was a *drachma,* a greek coin worth a day's wages (Luke 15:8).
4. *Tribute money* was a half shekel per person, and the *piece of money* that Peter found in the fish's mouth, a Greek *stater,* would have payed for two people (Matt. 17:24-27).
5. The man who owned the vineyard in Jesus' parable gave each laborer a *denarius* (penny in KJV), a Roman coin worth about one day's wages (Matt. 20:1,2).
6. The widow's mite was a Jewish *lepton* (mite in KJV). It was worth half a *kodrantes* (farthing in KJV) and could be used in the temple because it did not picture a pagan deity (Mark 12:42).

101. Three Cases of Extortion

1. Jacob would not feed Esau until he could extract a promise from Esau to give up his birthright (Gen. 25:29-34).
2. Samson's wedding guests threatened his wife, saying, "Entice thy husband, that he may declare unto us the riddle, lest we burn thee and thy father's house with fire" (Judges 14:15).
3. The sons of Eli threatened to take the uncooked sacrificial meat by force unless those who brought it gave it to them (1 Sam. 2:12-17).

102. Five Bribes

1. The lords of the Philistines each offered Delilah eleven hundred pieces of silver if she would find the secret of Samson's strength and tell them (Judges 16:5).
2. "When Samuel was old, . . . his sons walked not in his ways, but turned aside after lucre, and took bribes, and perverted judgment" (1 Sam. 8:1-3).

3. Judas Iscariot was given thirty pieces of silver to betray Jesus (Matt. 26:14-16).
4. The chief priests bribed the guards of Jesus' tomb to say that the disciples had stolen the body (Matt. 28:11-15).
5. Felix kept Paul in prison, hoping that Paul would bribe him for release (Acts 24:26).

14

People to People

Almost every community has a recluse; surely you must remember at least one. The old man who lived by himself back in the woods in an old dingy house, and only came to town when he was in need of food. The old lady who lived down the street in the foreboding dark house and was only seen when peering out from behind the curtains. Like Howard Hughes, at some time in life they decided to shut themselves off from others and try to find happiness by themselves. Unfortunately, the recluse's life becomes one marked by eccentricity and extreme unhappiness.

Life will not be fulfilling if we try to avoid the reality of people around us. It is necessary and good that we interact with each other. It is the way of growth and maturity. Interaction with others will create difficult situations. Just as love is the fruit of interacting with others, so are anger and people who are difficult to be with. These are all a part of maturing. The following lists include some of the interpersonal relationships we will find ourselves in: times of hugs and kisses, times of people being angry, getting to know the mothers-in-law, competition with each other, and the drawing of contracts in business relationships.

103. Thirteen Contracts

1. Abimelech swore to Abraham that the well dug by Abraham would not be bothered by his men. Abraham gave him seven ewe lambs as a witness of the deal (Gen. 21:25-32).
2. Abraham purchased a burial plot for Sarah from Ephron the Hittite. He had to pay 400 shekels of silver for the deed (Gen. 23:10-20).

3. Jacob forced the starving Esau to swear over his birthright before Jacob would feed him any pottage (Gen. 25:29-34).
4. Jacob negotiated a work contract with Laban. He would take no wages, but only the striped, spotted, and speckled sheep from Laban's flocks. The Lord blessed Laban with many striped, spotted, and speckled lambs (Gen. 30:29-43).
5. Laban and Jacob later set up a stone pillar to witness a contract of peace between them (Gen. 31:44-53).
6. Joseph's brothers sold him to slave traders for twenty shekels of silver (Gen. 37:28).
7. The lords of the Philistines each offered Delilah eleven hundred pieces of silver if she would find out the secret of Samson's strength for them (Judges 16:4,5).
8. Micah hired a Levite to be a priest in his shrine for an annual salary of ten shekels and a suit of clothing (Judges 17:10).
9. Ruth's closest relative gave Boaz the right to buy Naomi's property and to marry Ruth and then confirmed the agreement by removing his shoe (Ruth 4:1-10).
10. David pledged kindness to Jonathan and his family with an oath. He later fulfilled his oath by caring for Jonathan's son Mephibosheth (1 Sam. 20:12-17; 2 Sam. 9:6-7).
11. Solomon contracted with Hiram for the use of his servants. Hiram's men would cut cedar for the temple and Solomon would pay their wages (1 Kings 5:2-12).
12. King Ben-hadad of Syria promised King Ahab the return of all the Samarian cities taken by his father in return for his safe release (1 Kings 20:34).
13. Jeremiah bought a field from Hananeel his cousin for seventeen shekels of silver. The payment and signing of the deed was all done before witnesses (Jer. 32:6-12).

104. Fourteen Censuses

1. The population of the Garden of Eden was one until God doubled it (Gen. 2:8,22).
2. The post-Flood census showed only eight survivors (1 Pet. 3:20).
3. The Israelites numbered seventy-five when they went into the land of Egypt (Acts 7:14).
4. Six-hundred thousand men (plus women and children) left Egypt on foot in the Exodus (Ex. 12:37).

Joseph is sold to Midianite traders

5. God commanded Moses to number his army by recording every male twenty years old or older (Num. 1:1-46). The results were:
The tribe of Reuben—46,500
The tribe of Simeon—59,300
The tribe of Gad—45,650

The tribe of Judah—74,600
The tribe of Issachar—54,400
The tribe of Zebulun—57,400
The half tribe of Ephraim—40,500
The half tribe of Manasseh—32,200
The tribe of Benjamin—35,400
The tribe of Dan—62,700
The tribe of Asher—41,500
The tribe of Naphtali—53,400
Total number of Israelite fighting men—603,550

6. God also commanded that a census be taken of the Levites. Moses found 22,000 Levites more than one month old (Num. 3:39).
7. After 24,000 had died in a plague of judgment, God again commanded Moses to number the army. Moses found 601,730 men over twenty years of age (Num. 26:1-51).
8. The armies of Israel came against the tribe of Benjamin in judgment. A numbering of the armies showed 26,000 Benjamite soldiers and 400,000 from Israel. After the battle, only 600 Benjamite men remained (Judges 20:14-48).
9. Saul numbered the army that had gathered to fight the Ammonites and he counted 330,000 men (1 Sam. 11:8).
10. David brought God's wrath upon Israel by numbering the kingdom. He counted 1,300,000 "valiant men that drew the sword." God sent a plague that killed 70,000 of those men in one day (2 Sam. 24:1-15).
11. Under King David "the Levites were numbered from the age of thirty years and upward: and their number by their polls, man by man was 38,000" (1 Chron. 23:3).
12. "And Solomon numbered all the [aliens] in the land of Israel . . . and they were found 153,600" (2 Chron. 2:17).
13. Ezra brought 42,360 people and 7,337 of their servants back to Jerusalem from Babylon (Ezra 2:64,65).
14. "And it came to pass in those days, that there went out a decree from Caesar Augustus, that all the world should be [enrolled]" (Luke 2:1).

105. Seventeen Hugs and Kisses

1. Isaac kissed Jacob thinking that he was Esau (Gen. 27:27).
2. Jacob kissed Rachel almost as soon as he met her. These kissing cousins were later wed (Gen. 29:11).

3. Laban embraced Jacob, kissed him, and brought him into his house (Gen. 29:13).
4. When Jacob and Laban parted company, Laban kissed his "sons and daughters and blessed them" (Gen. 31:55).
5. "Esau ran to meet [Jacob], and embraced him, and fell on his neck, and kissed him: and they wept" (Gen. 33:4).
6. Joseph kissed all his brothers and wept when they were reunited (Gen. 45:15).
7. Israel kissed, embraced, and blessed Ephraim and Manasseh, Joseph's sons (Gen. 48:10,20).
8. When Jacob died, "Joseph fell upon his father's face, and wept upon him, and kissed him" (Gen. 50:1).
9. Aaron "met Moses in the mount of God, and kissed him" (Ex. 4:27).
10. "Jethro, Moses' father-in-law, came . . . unto Moses into the wilderness, . . . and Moses went out to meet his father-in-law, and did obeisance, and kissed him" (Ex. 18:5,7).
11. Naomi kissed Orpah and Ruth, her daughters-in-law, as she left them to return to her own country (Ruth 1:9).

Naomi kisses her daughters-in-law good-bye

12. "Samuel took a vial of oil, and poured it upon [Saul's] head, and kissed him, and said, Is it not because the Lord hath anointed thee to be captain over his inheritance?" (1 Sam. 10:1).
13. David and Jonathan kissed one another and wept when David began his flight from Saul (1 Sam. 20:41).
14. After Absalom's two years in exile, he returned to his father and King David kissed him (2 Sam. 14:33).
15. "When any man came nigh to Absalom to do him obeisance, he put forth his hand, and took him, and kissed him. . . . So Absalom stole the hearts of the men of Israel" (2 Sam. 15:5,6).
16. When David returned to Jerusalem from fighting Absalom, he met and kissed Barzillai, an old man who had provided supplies for David's army (2 Sam. 19:39).
17. "Joab took Amasa by the beard with the right hand to kiss him. But Amasa took no heed to the sword that was in Joab's hand: so [Joab] smote him therewith . . . and he died" (2 Sam. 20:9,10).

106. Late Night Visitors

1. Jacob was met by *a man* whom he wrestled all night. He later realized that the "man" was actually God (Gen. 32:22-31).
2. The *angel of death* came through Egypt at midnight (Ex. 12:29-31).
3. *Gideon* and his *three hundred men* attacked the Midianite camp at night (Judges 7:19).
4. *The Lord* came to Samuel at night (1 Sam. 4:1-14).
5. *David* and *Abishai* visited Saul's camp at night and took Saul's spear and a jug of water (1 Sam. 26:7-12).
6. *King Saul* visited the witch of Endor at night (1 Sam. 28:8).
7. The *shepherds* in Bethlehem were visited by a host of angels while they watched their flocks at night. After the news of the Messiah's birth had been revealed, *they* went to visit Joseph, Mary, and Jesus (Luke 2:8-16).
8. "About the fourth watch of the night [Jesus] cometh unto them, walking upon the sea" (Mark 6:48).
9. "There was a man of the Pharisees named *Nicodemus,* a ruler of the Jews: the same came to Jesus at night" (John 3:1,2).

Jacob wrestles with God

10. "*Judas* then, having received a band of men and officers from the chief priests and Pharisees, cometh thither with lanterns and torches and weapons.... Then the band and the captain and officers of the Jews took Jesus, and bound him" (John 18:3,12).

11. An *angel* came to Peter late at night and released him from

prison, and then *Peter* went to visit a prayer meeting at the home of John Mark's mother (Acts 12:6-17).

12. Paul was visited by an *angel* one night who assured him that all on board the storm-tossed boat would be safe (Acts 27:23,24).

107. Angry Brothers

1. "Cain rose up against Abel his brother, and slew him" (Gen. 4:8).
2. "Esau hated Jacob because of the blessing wherewith his father blessed him: and Esau said, . . . I will slay my brother Jacob" (Gen. 27:41).
3. The sons of Jacob were very angry when they heard that Shechem had raped their sister Dinah (Gen. 34:7).
4. "And when [Joseph's] brethren saw that their father loved him more than all his brethren, they hated him, and could not speak peaceably unto him" (Gen. 37:4).
5. Moses came down the mountain and saw the golden calf that Aaron his brother had made. He angrily rebuked Aaron for causing the people to sin (Ex. 32:19-22).
6. Abimelech, the son of Gideon, killed all seventy of his brothers at once (Judges 9:1-5).
7. Jephthah was thrown out of the house by his brothers because he was an illegitimate son of their father (Judges 11:1,2).
8. Eliab, David's oldest brother, was angered by David's concern over Goliath's challenge. He said that David had come out just to see the fighting (1 Sam. 17:28-30).
9. "Absalom hated his [brother] Ammon, because he had forced his sister Tamar" (2 Sam. 13:22).
10. The prodigal son's older brother was angry and would not go in to the prodigal's welcome-home party (Luke 15:28).

108. Eight Important Mothers-in-law

1. Sarah was Rebekah's mother-in-law (Gen. 21:3; 24:67).
2. Rebekah was Leah and Rachel's mother-in-law (Gen. 27:46; 29:21-28).
3. Moses' mother Jochebed was Zipporah's mother-in-law (Ex. 2:21; Num. 26:59).
4. Naomi was Ruth and Orpah's mother-in-law (Ruth 1:14).

5. King Saul's wife Ahinoam was David's mother-in-law (1 Sam. 14:50; 18:27).
6. Queen Jezebel was the mother-in-law of King Jehoram (1 Kings 21:4,5; 2 Kings 8:16-18).
7. Queen Athaliah was the mother-in-law of Ahaziah's wife Zibiah (2 Chron. 22:10-12; 24:1).
8. Peter's mother-in-law was healed of a fever by Jesus (Matt. 8:14,15).

109. Six Important Contests

1. Rachel and Leah competed for Jacob's love. They sought to have children to earn his favor (Gen. 30:1).
2. Moses and the magicians of Egypt competed in doing miracles. They all turned their rods into snakes, but Moses' ate up the other snakes (Ex. 7:10-12).
3. Korah questioned Moses' authority so Moses had Aaron and Korah take censers of incense before the Lord to see whom God would accept. Korah lost by default. A fiery crevice opened and swallowed Korah and his men before the contest could be completed (Num. 16:16-35).
4. God commanded each tribe to bring a rod and set it before him in the tabernacle overnight. Aaron's rod blossomed and thus proved that Aaron was God's chosen high priest (Num. 17:1-13).
5. Elijah challenged the priests of Baal to a contest to prove who the true God really was. Jehovah sent fire down from heaven to consume Elijah's sacrifice, including the altar (1 Kings 18:25-39).
6. The soldiers cast lots for Jesus' garments (Matt. 27:35).

15

The Animal World

"Look over there—it's a deer!" Such exclamations remind us of the wonder of the zoological kingdom. Other phrases like, "Beware of the dogs," remind us that though the animal world is wondrous, we still need to be careful. The stories of tourists being attacked by bears in Yellowstone National Park, or of a local farmer being gored by his prize bull, keep us wary.

The Bible recounts the creation of animals and is saturated with stories about, or including, animals. Many of the accounts include the enchantment that the animal world provides; other accounts include the danger that exists. Both elements are found in these lists. The lists also hold interest for those avid fishermen seeking new techniques for larger catches. There is even a section for those interested in the study of worms.

110. Five Animals That Attacked People

1. Two she *bears* attacked a group of children (2 Kings 2:24).
2. God sent *hornets* before Israel to drive away the Amorites (Josh. 24:12).
3. A young *lion* attacked Samson (Judges 14:5).
4. Jonah was swallowed by a *whale* (Matt. 12:40).
5. Paul was bitten by a *viper* on the island of Melita (Acts 28:3).

111. Monsters

1. "Behold now *behemoth* which I made with thee; he eateth grass as an ox" (Job 40:15).
2. "In the habitation of *dragons,* where each lay, shall be grass with reeds and rushes" (Isa. 35:7).
3. "The Lord with his sore and great and strong sword shall punish *leviathan* the piercing serpent" (Isa. 27:1).
4. "Even the *sea monsters* . . . give suck to their young ones" (Lam. 4:3).
5. The Lord "hath as it were the strength of an *unicorn*" (Num. 23:22).

112. Three Catches of Fish

1. Jesus told Peter to take the first fish that he caught and open its mouth. He would find a coin there to pay tribute for both Jesus and himself (Matt. 17:24-27).
2. When Jesus commanded Peter to launch out into the deep and drop his nets, Peter reminded Him of the poor fishing the previous night. Nevertheless, Peter obeyed and caught enough fish to fill two boats (Luke 5:1-7).
3. Peter was again fishing unsuccessfully when Jesus yelled out from the shore, telling him to cast his net on the other side of the boat. Peter did that and caught 153 large fish (John 21:2-11).

113. Worms

1. "Some of them left [the manna] until the morning, and it bred *worms,* and stank" (Ex. 16:20).
2. "That which the *palmerworm* hath left hath the locust eaten; and that which the locust hath left hath the *cankerworm* eaten; and that which the cankerworm hath left hath the *caterpillar* eaten" (Joel 1:4).
3. Job said, "My flesh is clothed with *worms* and clods of dust" (Job 7:5).
4. "The Lord God prepared a gourd, and made it to come up over Jonah. . . . But God prepared a *worm* when the morning rose the next day, and it smote the gourd that it withered" (Jonah 4:6,7).

An artist's concept of leviathan

5. "The nations shall see and be confounded. . . . They shall lick the dust like a serpent, they shall move out of their holes like *worms* of the earth" (Mic. 7:16,17).
6. Jesus said that hell is a place where the "*worm* dieth not" (Mark 9:43,44).

7. 'The angel of the Lord smote [Herod], because he gave not God the glory and he was eaten of *worms,* and gave up the ghost" (Acts 12:23).

114. Snakes

1. "And the Lord God said unto the serpent, Because thou hast done this [beguiled Eve to eat the forbidden fruit], . . . upon thy belly shalt thou go" (Gen. 3:14,15).
2. In blessing his sons, Jacob said, "Dan shall be a serpent by the way, an adder in the path, that biteth the horse heels, so that his rider shall fall backward" (Gen. 49:17).
3. Moses' rod became a serpent when he cast it on the ground (Ex. 4:2-4).
4. "The people spake against God, and against Moses. . . . And the Lord sent fiery serpents among the people, and they bit the people; and much of Israel died" (Num. 21:5,6).
5. "The day of the Lord is darkness, and not light. As if a man did flee from a lion, and a bear met him; or went into the house, and leaned his hand on the wall, and a serpent bit him" (Amos 5:18,19).
6. Jesus said to His disciples, "Behold, I give unto you power to tread on serpents and scorpions, and over all the power of the enemy: and nothing shall by any means hurt you" (Luke 10:19).
7. "When Paul had gathered a bundle of sticks, and laid them on the fire, there came a viper out of the heat, and fastened on his hand" (Acts 28:3).

115. Important Donkeys

1. An ass carried the wood upon which Abraham was planning to sacrifice Isaac (Gen. 22:1-3).
2. Jacob gave Esau twenty she asses and ten foals to appease him (Gen. 32:13-18).
3. "Moses took his wife and his sons, and set them upon an ass, and returned to the land of Egypt" (Ex. 4:20).
4. Balaam's ass verbally rebuked him for harsh treatment (Num. 22:21-33).
5. Saul was looking for his father's lost asses when he met Samuel (1 Sam. 9:1-6).
6. Abigail rode an ass to plead with David for her husband's life (1 Sam. 25:20).

7. "Absalom rode upon a mule, and the mule went under the thick boughs of a great oak, and his head caught hold of the oak" (2 Sam. 18:9).
8. The Shunammite sent her servant on an ass to Elisha to tell him that her son had died (2 Kings 4:18-32).
9. Jesus rode into Jerusalem on an ass (Matt. 21:1-9).

16

Transportation

The Bible lists that follow explore some of the transportation methods used in ancient days. The standard cart and chariots were no match for today's freeway traffic, but they certainly were economical. There are at least three methods of transportation in the lists that may be well worth our exploring as an alternative to the "gas hog" we may be driving. Check the economy rating on the following modes of travel: the chariot of fire that transported Elijah to heaven, the chariots that Zechariah saw being driven by angels, and the speedy trip that Philip made after baptizing the Ethiopian eunuch. If you could only get somebody to duplicate these, you'd be a millionaire.

116. Important Carts and Chariots

1. "Pharaoh said unto Joseph, See, I have set thee over all the land of Egypt. . . . And he made him to ride in the second chariot which he had" (Gen. 41:41,43).
2. Joseph sent wagons to Canaan to carry back his father and his brothers' families (Gen. 45:17-21).
3. "The Egyptians pursued after [the Israelites with] all the horses and chariots of Pharaoh" (Ex. 14:9).
4. The Levites were given six covered wagons in which to haul the tabernacle and its furnishings (Num. 7:1-9).
5. The Philistines sent the Ark of the Covenant back to the Israelites on a cart pulled by a cow (1 Sam. 6:7-14).
6. "Solomon . . . had a thousand and four hundred chariots" (1 Kings 10:26).

7. King Rehoboam's tax gatherer was stoned, so Rehoboam sped away to the safety of Jerusalem in his chariot (1 Kings 12:18).

8. King Ahab rode into battle in a chariot but was fatally hit by an Assyrian arrow (1 Kings 22:34-38).

9. "There appeared a chariot of fire, and horses of fire . . . and Elijah went up by a whirlwind into heaven" (2 Kings 2:11).

10. "Naaman came with his horses and with his chariot, and stood at the door of the house of Elisha" waiting to be healed of his leprosy (2 Kings 5:9).

11. The Lord sent many horses and chariots of fire to guard the Israelites against the invading Syrians (2 Kings 6:14-17).

12. Jehu rode in a chariot and chased the chariots of King Ahaziah and King Joram and killed them both (2 Kings 9:16-28).

13. While wiping out idolatry in the land, King Josiah burned the chariots of the sun (2 Kings 23:11).

14. King Josiah was wounded while fighting the Egyptians, so his servants took him from his own chariot "and put him in the second chariot that he had; and they brought him to Jerusalem, and he died" (2 Chron. 35:23,24).

A king on his chariot

15. Zechariah saw four chariots driven by angels (Zech. 6:1-8).
16. The Ethiopian eunuch was riding back to Ethiopia in a chariot when Philip came upon him (Acts 8:27,28).

117. The Longest Journeys in the Bible

1. Abraham moved his entire household from Haran to Canaan (Gen. 12:1-5).
2. Israel wandered through the wilderness for forty years after they had left Egypt to go to the Promised Land (Deut. 29:5).
3. Jesus' longest journey, made when He was a baby, was from Bethlehem to Egypt (Matt. 2:14).
4. Jesus' longest journey during His ministry was from Capernaum to Jerusalem (Matt. 17:24; 20:17).
5. The Ethiopian eunuch rode by chariot from Ethiopia to Jerusalem and back (Acts 8:27).

118. The Fastest Travelers in the Bible

1. Elijah raced Ahab's chariot on foot between Mount Carmel and Samaria and won (1 Kings 18:44-46).
2. The Spirit caught Philip away from the eunuch and took him to Azotus (Acts 8:39,40).

17

Forces of Nature

Through the advances of meteorology, we are able to watch the development of weather patterns every evening on the local TV news. It's fascinating to be able to watch the satellite pictures of the cloud cover and the radar images of rain and wind fronts. Somehow one gets the sense that we actually understand what is happening in nature. We can easily forget that, though we may now understand more about what is happening in nature, we still have no say about what happens. We still find ourselves extremely vulnerable to the powers of the wind, rain, snow, floods, etc.

The following lists show that the people in the Bible were also very vulnerable to nature's forces. In these lists, we see not only the powerful weather patterns that the writers observed, but the ways in which God was often very active in using these patterns for His purposes. Recorded are many instances when God intervened via strong winds, hail, floods, lightning, thunder, and rain. He used these methods to speak to people then, and we shouldn't be surprised if He uses them to speak to us today.

119. Thunder and Lightning

1. Thunder and lightning accompanied the veil of clouds that hung around Mount Sinai when God gave Moses the law (Ex. 19:16).
2. "The Philistines drew near to do battle against Israel: but the Lord thundered with a great thunder on that day upon the Philistines, and discomfited them" (1 Sam. 7:10).
3. "Samuel called unto the Lord; and the Lord sent thunder

and rain that day: and all the people greatly feared the Lord and Samuel" (1 Sam. 12:18).

4. John saw thunder and lightning before the Lord poured out His wrath upon the earth (Rev. 11:19).

120. Three Tornadoes (Whirlwinds)

1. "Elijah went up by a whirlwind into heaven" (2 Kings 2:11).
2. "The Lord answered Job out of the whirlwind" (Job 38:1).
3. Ezekiel "looked, and behold, a whirlwind came out of the north, a great cloud, and a fire infolding itself" (Ezek. 1:4).

121. Three Important Rainstorms

1. "The rain was upon the earth forty days and nights" while Noah was in the ark (Gen. 7:12).
2. "Samuel called unto the Lord; and the Lord sent thunder and rain that day" (1 Sam. 12:18).
3. After three-and-a-half years of devastating drought in Israel, Elijah prayed for rain and it came again (1 Kings 18:45).

122. Weather Miracles

1. The Lord sent fire and hail upon the Egyptians, but He spared the land of Goshen where the Israelites lived (Ex. 9:22-33).
2. "The Lord turned a mighty strong wind, which took away the locusts, and cast them into the Red sea" (Ex. 10:19).
3. As the Amorites fled before Israel, "the Lord cast down great stones from heaven upon them unto Azekah, and they died" (Josh. 10:11).
4. "Samuel called unto the Lord; and the Lord sent thunder and rain that day" (1 Sam. 12:18).
5. Elijah "prayed earnestly that it might not rain: and it rained not on the earth by the space of three years and six months. And he prayed again, and the heaven gave rain" (James 5:17,18).
6. Jonah's ship was hit by a mighty tempest that died down as soon as he was thrown overboard (Jonah 1:3-16).
7. The disciples were out on the Sea of Galilee in a storm when Jesus came to them walking on the water. When He got into the boat, the wind stopped (Matt. 14:24,33).

Jonah is thrown overboard to quell the storm

8. Jesus "rebuked the wind, and said unto the sea, Peace, be still. And the wind ceased, and there was a great calm" (Mark 4:39).

123. Earthquakes

1. As the Israelites waited before Mount Sinai, the Lord descended and the whole mountain quaked (Ex. 19:18).
2. Jonathan came against a Philistine garrison, and an earthquake accompanied his attack (1 Sam. 14:14-15).
3. The Lord passed by Elijah and an earthquake followed (1 Kings 19:11,12).
4. "Jesus, when he had cried again with a loud voice, yielded up the ghost. And . . . the earth did quake" (Matt. 27:50,51).

5. "There was a great earthquake: for the angel of the Lord descended from heaven, and came and rolled back the stone from the door" (Matt. 28:2).

6. Paul and Silas were in prison in Philippi when "suddenly there was a great earthquake, so that the foundations of the prison were shaken" (Acts 16:26).

7. Jesus declared that earthquakes in "divers places" would come before the end of the world (Matt. 24:7).

18

Violence

Leo Tolstoy wrote concerning mankind, "A good portion of the evils that afflict mankind is due to the erroneous belief that life can be made secure by violence." Ever since the day that Cain slew Abel, violence as a means to gain something has been a way of life. Today we live in a generation when nothing seems to shock us. On the evening news, we watch bank robbers shooting their hostages; we watch the daily bloodshed of warfare from some part of the world; we watch the riots and looting in foreign cities. We are being conditioned to violence.

The human race has not changed much over the last 2,000 years. The following lists show some of the acts of violence which took place during Bible times. Remember Coue's glowing statement from the late nineteenth century, "Every day in every way, I am getting better and better." It became a symbol of where mankind thought they were heading. I wonder what he would say today.

124. Five Riots

1. The people of Nazareth "rose up, and thrust Jesus out of the city, and led him unto the brow of the hill whereon their city was built, that they might cast him down headlong" (Luke 4:29).
2. Pilate bowed to the wishes of the crowd and allowed Jesus to be crucified because the mob had become uncontrollable (Matt. 27:23,24).
3. The unbelieving Thessalonian Jews "took unto them certain lewd fellows of the baser sort, and gathered a company,

and set all the city on an uproar, and assaulted the house of Jason, and sought to bring them out [Paul and Silas] to the people" (Acts 17:5).

4. The Ephesians "were full of wrath, and cried out, saying, Great is Diana of the Ephesians. And the whole city was filled with confusion: . . . they rushed with one accord into the theatre" (Acts 19:28,29).

5. All Jerusalem "was moved, and the people ran together: and they took Paul, and drew him out of the temple. . . . He was borne of the soldiers for the violence of the people" (Acts 21:30-35).

125. Three Ambushes

1. Joshua drew the army of Ai out of the city while another group ambushed and destroyed the city (Josh. 8:12-22).

2. The armies of Israel drew the Benjamites out of the city of Gibeah by retreating before them. But more Israelites were lurking behind the city and they ambushed Gibeah (Judges 20:29-43).

3. More than forty men were waiting in ambush for Paul, but the Roman soldiers moved him secretly out of Jerusalem at night (Acts 23:21-23).

126. Defensive Weapons

1. Goliath "had an *helmet of brass* upon his head, and he was armed with a *coat of mail*; and the weight of the coat was five thousand shekels of brass. And he had *greaves of brass* upon his legs, and a *target of brass* between his shoulders" (1 Sam. 17:4-6).

2. "Uzziah prepared for them throughout all the host *shields,* and spears, and *helmets,* and *habergeons,* and bows, and slings to cast stones. And he made in Jerusalem *engines,* invented by cunning men to be on the towers and upon the bulwarks, to shoot arrows and great stones withal" (2 Chron. 26:14,15).

3. "Order ye the *buckler* and *shield,* and draw near to battle. Harness the horses; and get up, ye horsemen, and stand forth with your *helmets*; furbish the spears, and put on the *brigandines*" (Jer. 46:3,4).

127. Offensive Weapons

1. David "took his *staff* in his hand, and chose him five smooth *stones* out of the brook, and put them in a shepherd's bag which he had, even in a scrip; and his *sling* was in his hand" (1 Sam. 17:40).
2. "'And Saul cast the *javelin*; for he said, I will smite David even to the wall with it" (1 Sam. 18:11).
3. David's men "were armed with *bows,* and could use both the right hand and the left in hurling *stones* and shooting *arrows* out of a *bow*" (1 Chron. 12:2).
4. Hezekiah "strengthened himself, . . . and made *darts* and shields in abundance" (2 Chron. 32:5).
5. "A man that beareth false witness against his neighbour is a *maul,* and a *sword,* and a sharp *arrow*" (Prov. 25:18).
6. Ezekiel was commanded to make a model of Jerusalem and "set *battering rams* against it round about" (Ezek. 4:1,2).
7. "One of the soldiers with a *spear* pierced his side" (John 19:34).

128. Murder Weapons and Devices

1. Ehud killed King Eglon of Moab with a two-edged *dagger* (Judges 3:16-21).
2. Joab "took three *darts* in his hand, and thrust them through the heart of Absalom" (2 Sam. 18:14).
3. Hazel "took a *thick cloth,* and dipped it in water, and spread it on [Ben-hadad's] face, so that he died" (2 Kings 8:15).
4. Adrammelech and Sharezer killed their father Sennácherib with a *sword* (2 Kings 19:37).
5. "King Rehoboam sent Hadoram that was over the tribute; and the children of Israel stoned him with *stones* that he died" (2 Chron. 10:18).

129. Unusual Weapons

1. "Shamgar . . . slew of the Philistines six hundred men with an *ox goad*" (Judges 3:31).
2. "Jael Heber's wife took a *nail of the tent,* and took an *hammer* in her hand, and went softly unto [Sisera], and smote the nail into his temple, and fastened it into the ground" (Judges 4:17-21).

3. Samson "found a new *jawbone of an ass,* and put forth his hand, and took it, and slew a thousand men therewith" (Judges 15:15).
4. "The staff of [Goliath's] spear was like a weaver's beam; and his spear's head weighed six hundred shekels of iron" (1 Sam. 17:7).

The death of Sisera

19

Death and Funerals

Shakespeare devoted much thought, in writing his plays, to the theme of death. In the play *King Henry VI*, he wrote these words: "Why, what is pomp, rule, reign, but earth and dust? And live we how we can, yet die we must." His characters are often made to face the issue of death, and many of them die tragically. In contrast, our Western society provides little in the way of preparation for death. It is an issue that most of us would rather not think or talk about. Shakespeare is correct, though—"yet die we must."

The following Bible lists show deaths and funerals of the people of that time. Some of the deaths recorded followed lives filled with corruption and wrongdoing. Some followed lives lived for the glory of God. In either case the sadness of the loss of a loved one was always there, but in the case of a righteous life there was always the great anticipation of the resurrection from the dead. Paul's words are always timely: "For me to live is Christ, to die is gain." He saw death as a mere stepping into eternal life with Christ.

How we view death will profoundly affect how we live. Death in the Bible is never seen as the end of life, but rather, as an entrance into eternity. As Catherine Booth declared on her deathbed, "The waters are rising but I am not sinking."

130. Nineteen Graves and Graveyards

1. "But Deborah Rebekah's nurse died, and she was buried beneath Beth-el under an oak: and the name of it was called Allon-bachuth" (Gen. 35:8).

2. "Rachel died, and was buried in the way to Ephrath, which is Bethlehem. And Jacob set a pillar upon her grave" (Gen. 35:19,20).

3. Abraham, Sarah, Isaac, Rebekah, Jacob, and Leah were all buried in the cave of the field of Machpelah before Mamre (Gen. 49:30,31; 50:13).

4. The Lord buried Moses "in a valley in the land of Moab, over against Beth-peor: but no man knoweth of his sepulchre unto this day" (Deut. 34:6).

5. A heap of stones was raised over the bodies of Achan and his family after they were stoned in the valley of Achor (Josh. 7:25,26).

6. The Israelites took the body of the king of Ai "and cast it at the entering of the gate of the city, and [raised] thereon a great heap of stones" (Josh. 8:29).

7. Israel buried Joshua "in the border of his inheritance in Timnath-serah" (Josh. 24:30).

8. "The bones of Joseph, which the children of Israel brought up out of Egypt, buried they in Shechem" (Josh. 24:32).

9. "Gideon the son of Joash died in a good old age, and was buried in the sepulchre of Joash his father" (Judges 8:32).

10. Samson was buried "between Zorah and Eshtaol in the burying place of Manoah his father" (Judges 16:31).

11. The men of Jabesh-gilead "took the body of Saul and the bodies of his sons from the wall of Beth-shan, and came to Jabesh, and burnt them there. And they took their bones, and buried them under a tree at Jabesh" (1 Sam. 31:12,13).

12. "Samuel died; and all the Israelites were gathered together, and lamented him, and buried him in his house at Ramah" (1 Sam. 25:1).

13. Joab "took Absalom, and cast him into a great pit in the wood, and laid a very great heap of stones upon him" (2 Sam. 18:17).

14. King Jehoram was killed by Jehu, and his body was cast into Naboth's field (2 Kings 9:25).

15. Ahaziah's servants "buried him in his sepulchre with his fathers in the city of David" (2 Kings 9:28).

16. "Manasseh slept with his fathers, and was buried in the garden of his own house, in the garden of Uzza" (2 Kings 21:18).

17. Amon "was buried in his sepulchre in the garden of Uzza" (2 Kings 21:26).

152

18. "Uzziah slept with his fathers, and they buried him with his fathers in the field of the burial which belonged to the kings; for they said, He is a leper" (2 Chron. 26:23).
19. "And the chief priests took the silver pieces. . . . And they took counsel, and bought with them the potter's field, to bury strangers" (Matt. 27:6,7).

131. Executions

1. The Roman soldiers crucified Jesus along with two common criminals at the demand of the Jews (Matt. 27:33-50).

Samuel executes Agag

2. Pharaoh "hanged the chief baker" (Gen. 40:22).
3. The Levites executed 3,000 men for worshiping the golden calf (Ex. 32:26-28).
4. Joshua hung the king of Ai (Josh. 8:28,20).
5. Joshua executed Adoni-zedec, king of Jerusalem; Hoham, king of Hebron; Piram, king of Jarmuth; Japhia, king of Lachish; and Debir, king of Eglon (Josh. 10:1-26).
6. "Samuel hewed Agag [the king of the Amalekites] in pieces before the Lord in Gilgal" (1 Sam. 15:33).
7. King Saul ordered Doeg to execute eighty-five priests of the Lord (1 Sam. 22:17,18).
8. David executed a young Amalekite for claiming that he had killed King Saul (2 Sam. 1:6-15).
9. David ordered his men to kill Rechab and Baanah because they had murdered Ishbosheth, Saul's son (2 Sam. 4:9-12).
10. The Gibeonites hung seven of Saul's grandsons in retribution for one of Saul's bloody actions against them (2 Sam. 21:1-9).
11. At King Solomon's command, Benaiah executed Adonijah, Joab, and Shimei (1 Kings 2:25,34,46).
12. King Ahasuerus hung his chamberlains, Bigthan and Teresh (Esther 2:21,23).
13. King Ahasuerus also hung Haman on Haman's own gallows (Esther 7:5-10).
14. Haman's ten sons were hung at Esther's request (Esther 9:13,14).
15. King Jehoiakim executed the prophet Uriah for giving unfavorable prophecies (Jer. 26:20-23).
16. See list number 217—Successful and Attempted Stonings in *Meredith's Book of Bible Lists,* page 266.

132. Unusual Funeral Processions

1. The longest funeral procession was for Joseph. The Israelites carried his body for over forty years through the wilderness from Egypt to Canaan (Josh. 24:32).
2. The shortest funeral procession never made it to the cemetery. The young man of Nain was raised from his funeral bier by Jesus as the procession left the city (Luke 7:11-16).

133. Laws of Purification After Death

1. "He that toucheth the dead body of any man shall be unclean seven days. He shall purify himself with [the ashes of a red heifer] on the third day, then the seventh day he shall ... be clean (Num. 19:11,12).
2. "This is the law, when a man dieth in a tent: all that come into the tent, and all that is in the tent, shall be unclean seven days. . . . And a clean person shall take hyssop and dip it in the water, and sprinkle it upon the tent, and upon all the vessels, and upon the persons that were there" (Num. 19:14-18).

134. People Killed by Animals

1. "The Lord sent fiery serpents among the people, and they bit the people; and much people of Israel died" (Num. 21:6).
2. A disobedient prophet was killed by a lion along the path on which he was traveling (1 Kings 13:20-32).
3. Another lion killed a man who would not strike a young prophet with a sword as he had been commanded by the Lord to do (1 Kings 20:35,36).
4. A group of children made fun of Elisha, "and there came forth two she bears out of the wood, and tare forty and two children" (2 Kings 2:24).
5. "At the beginning of their dwelling there, . . . they [foreigners who had moved into Samaria] feared not the Lord: therefore the Lord sent lions among them, which slew some of them" (2 Kings 17:24,25).
6. "The king commanded, and they brought those men which had accused Daniel, and they cast them into the den of lions, them, their children, and their wives; and the lions had the mastery of them" (Dan. 6:24).

135. The Ten Largest Mass Deaths

1. "Abijah and his people slew them with a great slaughter: so there fell down slain of Israel five hundred thousand chosen men" (2 Chron. 13:17).
2. "The angel of the Lord went out, and smote in the camp of the Assyrians an hundred fourscore and five thousand" (2 Kings 19:35).

The man who disobeyed a prophet is killed by a lion

3. Gideon and his men killed 120,000 Midianites (Judges 8:10).

4. King Pekah killed 20,000 men of Judah in one day because they had forsaken the Lord (2 Chron. 28:6).

5. "The children of Israel slew of the Syrians an hundred thousand footmen in one day" (1 Kings 20:29).

6. "The other Jews that were in the king's provinces gathered themselves together, . . . and slew of their foes seventy and five thousand" (Esther 9:15,16).

7. "The Lord sent a pestilence upon Israel from the morning even to the time appointed: and there died of the people from Dan to Beersheba seventy thousand men" (2 Sam. 24:15).

8. The Lord "smote the men of Beth-shemesh, because they had looked into the ark of the Lord, even he smote of the

people fifty thousand and three score and ten men" (1 Sam. 6:19).

9. "David slew of the Syrians seven thousand men which fought in chariots, and forty thousand footmen" (1 Chron. 19:18).

10. "The Philistines fought, . . . and there was a very great slaughter; for there fell of Israel thirty thousand footmen" (1 Sam. 4:10).

20

Interesting People

Over the past few years one of the most popular television themes has been that of discovering people who do unique things. The offshoot has been a number of programs which go anywhere to locate something that will catch the viewer's attention. The popularity of the *Guiness Book of Records* indicates that we enjoy hearing about people who do unique things. Regular publications in issues of the *Reader's Digest* under the heading of "My Most Unforgettable Character" also indicate the wide interest we have in people whom we will not forget for some particular reason.

Compiled below are seven Bible lists of interesting people. They are people who are still remembered for a particular reason. Something about their lives stands out as different from the ordinary. Especially interesting are the people who received their names from heavenly sources.

136. Five Insomniacs

1. Jacob said to Laban, "This twenty years have I been with thee; . . . in the day the drought consumed me, and the frost by night; and my sleep departed from my eyes" (Gen. 31:38,40).
2. On the night after Haman built a gallows for the purpose of hanging Mordecai, King Ahasuerus could not sleep (Esther 6:1).
3. The wicked "sleep not, except they have done mischief; and their sleep is taken away, unless they cause some to fall" (Prov. 4:16).

4. "Nebuchadnezzar dreamed dreams, wherewith his spirit was troubled, and his sleep brake from him" (Dan. 2:1).
5. While Daniel was in the lions' den, King Darius stayed up all night (Dan. 6:18).

137. Twenty-three References to Runners

1. Abraham ran to meet the Lord in the plains of Mamre (Gen. 18:1,2).
2. Abraham's servant ran to meet Rebekah (Gen. 24:17).
3. Laban ran to meet Abraham's servant at the well (Gen. 24:29).
4. "Jacob told Rachel that he was her father's brother, . . . and she ran and told her father" (Gen. 29:12).
5. When Jacob returned to his country, "Esau ran to meet him, and embraced him, and fell on his neck, and kissed him: and they wept" (Gen. 33:4).
6. Aaron ran into the midst of the congregation with incense to stay a plague (Num. 16:46-48).
7. Samson's mother ran to her husband Manoah to tell him that an angel had appeared to her a second time (Judges 13:10).
8. When the Lord called the child Samuel, he ran to Eli thinking that Eli had called him (1 Sam. 3:4,5).
9. A Benjamite man ran from the battlefield to tell Eli that the ark of the Lord had been captured by the Philistines (1 Sam. 4:12-18).
10. David ran toward the Philistine camp to meet Goliath and slew him (1 Sam. 17:48,49).
11. Joab sent Cushi to run to David with the news of Absalom's death. Ahimaaz later volunteered and, in spite of his late start, beat Cushi to David with the news (2 Sam. 18:19-23).
12. "Adonijah the son of Gaggith exalted himself, saying, I will be king: and he prepared him chariots and horsemen, and fifty men to run before him" (1 Kings 1:5).
13. Elijah "girded up his loins, and ran before Ahab to the entrance of Jezreel" (1 Kings 18:46).
14. Elisha ran after Elijah to accept the appointment as his successor (1 Kings 19:19-21).
15. Gehazi ran from Elisha to meet the Shunammite woman (2 Kings 4:25,26).
16. An angel told another angel to run to Zechariah and to

deliver him the message that Jerusalem would again be inhabited (Zech. 2:3,4).

17. One of the onlookers at Jesus' crucifixion ran and found a sponge to use for giving Jesus a drink (Matt. 27:46,48).

18. Mary Magdalene and the other Mary ran from the empty tomb to tell the disciples about it (Matt. 28:8).

19. When the Gadarene demoniac "saw Jesus afar off, he ran and worshipped him" (Mark 5:6).

20. People ran to hear Jesus teach and to see Him perform miracles (Mark 6:33,35).

21. Zacchaeus ran before the throng around Jesus and climbed up into a sycamore tree to see Him (Luke 19:4)

22. John outran Peter to see the empty tomb (John 20:4).

23. Philip ran to the Ethiopian eunuch's chariot (Acts 8:30).

138. Blind People

1. When the men of Sodom attacked Lot's house, the two angels "smote the men that were at the door of the house with blindness" (Gen. 19:11).

2. "When Isaac was old, . . . his eyes were dim, so that he could not see" (Gen. 27:1).

3. "The eyes of Israel were dim for age, so that he could not see" (Gen. 48:10).

4. "The Philistines took [Samson], and put out his eyes, and brought him down to Gaza" (Judges 16:21).

5. "Eli was ninety and eight years old; and his eyes were dim, that he could not see" (1 Sam. 4:15).

6. "Ahijah could not see; for his eyes were set by reason of his age" (1 Kings 14:4).

7. "Elisha prayed unto the Lord, and said, Smite [the Syrian army], I pray thee, with blindness. And he smote them with blindness" (2 Kings 6:18).

8. Nebuchadnezzar "put out Zedekiah's eyes, and bound him with chains to carry him to Babylon" (Jer. 39:7).

9. "Two blind men followed Jesus, crying, and saying, Thou son of David, have mercy on us. . . . Then touched he their eyes, saying, According to your faith be it unto you. And their eyes were opened" (Matt. 9:27-30).

10. Two blind men sat by the road and cried out to Jesus to have mercy on them. He restored their sight instantly (Matt. 20:30-34).

Zacchaeus in the sycamore tree

11. Jesus touched one blind man and the man said, "I see men as trees, walking." Jesus touched him again and he saw clearly (Mark 8:22-25).
12. Jesus healed a blind beggar named Bartimaeus near Jericho (Mark 10:46-52).
13. Jesus put mud on the eyes of one blind man and told him to go and wash in the pool of Siloam. He washed his eyes and saw again (John 9:1-7).

14. Saul was blind for three days after the Lord stopped him on the way to Damascus and spoke to him out of a great light (Acts 9:9).

15. Elymas the sorcerer stood against Paul and Barnabas as they told Sergius Paulus the Gospel. Paul pronounced God's judgment upon Elymas, and he immediately became blind (Acts 13:7-12).

139. Eighteen Sleepers

1. "And the Lord caused a deep sleep to fall upon *Adam,* and he slept: and he took one of his ribs" (Gen. 2:21).
2. God spoke to *Abram* while he was in a deep sleep (Gen. 15:12-16).
3. *Jacob* slept at Bethel and dreamed about angels (Gen. 28:11-15).
4. *Pharaoh* dreamed of cows and corn while he slept (Gen. 41:1-7).
5. "Jael Heber's wife took a nail of the tent, and took an hammer in her hand, and went softly unto [Sisera], and smote the nail into his temples . . . for he was fast asleep and weary" (Judges 4:21).
6. *Samson* slept while the Philistines cut off his hair (Judges 16:19).
7. David and Abishai sneaked into *Saul's* camp while he was asleep (1 Sam. 26:7).
8. *Uriah* slept at David's door while he was on leave from the battlefront (2 Sam. 11:9).
9. Elijah sarcastically suggested that *Baal* was asleep when Jezebel's priests could not get him to respond (1 Kings 18:27).
10. While *Nebuchadnezzar* slept, he had a troubling dream which he could not remember in the morning (Dan. 2:1-9).
11. *Jonah* slept in the bottom of the ship while it rolled in the storm (Jonah 1:5).
12. *Joseph* was sleeping when an angel of the Lord came to him in a dream (Matt. 2:13).
13. While the disciples sailed, *Jesus* fell asleep. A storm came and they anxiously woke Him up (Luke 8:23,24).
14. Jesus told the mourners that *Jairus' daughter* was not dead, but only sleeping (Luke 8:52).
15. While Jesus prayed in Gethsemane, His *disciples* slept (Luke 22:45).

16. *Peter* was sleeping between two soldiers in prison when an angel came to release him (Acts 12:6,7).
17. The *Philippian jailor* was awakened from a deep sleep by the earthquake that hit his prison (Acts 16:27).
18. *Eutychus* fell asleep and fell to the ground through a third-story window while Paul preached. Paul stopped the service long enough to raise him from the dead (Acts 20:9-12).

140. Laughers

1. "Abraham fell upon his face, and laughed, and said in his heart, Shall a child be born unto him that is an hundred years old? and shall Sarah, that is ninety years old, bear?" (Gen. 17:17).
2. When Sarah heard that she would have a son, she laughed (Gen. 18:10-12).
3. Hezekiah sent decrees that made an urgent plea for repentance "from city to city through the country of Ephraim and Manasseh even unto Zebulun: but they laughed them to scorn" (2 Chron. 30:10).
4. "When Sanballat the Horonite, and Tobiah the servant, the Ammonite, and Geshem the Arabian, heard [that Nehemiah and his group were going to rebuild Jerusalem], they laughed" (Neh. 2:19).
5. "When Jesus came into the ruler's house, and saw the minstrels and the people making a noise, he said unto them, Give place: for the maid is not dead, but sleepeth. And they laughed him to scorn" (Matt. 9:23,24).

141. Dancers

1. "Miriam the prophetess, the sister of Aaron, took a timbrel in her hand; and all the women went out after her with timbrels and with dances" (Ex. 15:20).
2. The children of Israel danced before the calf that Aaron made (Ex. 32:19).
3. After Jephthah's victory over the Ammonites, "his daughter came out to meet him with timbrels and with dances" (Judges 11:34).
4. The men of Benjamin took wives from among the dancers at Shiloh (Judges 21:20,23).
5. After David had returned from killing Goliath, the women

Jephthah is met by his dancing daughter

of Israel came out dancing with tabrets to meet Saul (1 Sam. 18:6,7).

6. When David finally caught up with the Amalekites, "they were spread abroad upon all the earth, eating and drinking, and dancing, because of all the great spoil that they had taken out of all the land of the Philistines" (1 Sam. 30:16-18).

7. When the ark of the Lord was brought into Jerusalem, "David danced before the Lord with all his might" (2 Sam. 6:14).

8. The daughter of Herodias so enchanted Herod with a dance at his birthday party that he promised her anything she wanted. She asked for the head of John the Baptist (Matt. 14:6-8).

9. When the prodigal son came back, his father held a feast with music and dancing (Luke 15:25).

142. People Named by God, Jesus, or Angels

1. God called His human creation Adam (Gen. 5:2).

2. "The angel of the Lord said to [Hagar], Behold, thou art with child and shalt bear a son, and shalt call his name Ishmael" (Gen. 16:11).

3. The Lord said, "Neither shall thy name be any more Abram, but thy name shall be Abraham" (Gen. 17:5).

4. God told Abraham, "Thou shalt not call her name Sarai, but Sarah shall her name be" (Gen. 17:15).

5. "God said, Sarah thy wife shall bear thee a son indeed; and thou shalt call his name Isaac" (Gen. 17:19).

6. The Lord declared, "Thy name shall be called no more Jacob, but Israel" (Gen. 32:28).

7. The Lord told David, "Behold, a son shall be born to thee, who shall be a man of rest; and I will give him a rest from all his enemies round about: for his name shall be Solomon" (1 Chron. 22:9).

8. The Lord commanded Isaiah to call his son Maher-shalal-hash-baz (Isa. 8:3).

9. Jeremiah said to Pashur, "The Lord hath not called thy name Pashur, but Magor-missabib" (Jer. 20:3).

10. When Hosea had a son, the Lord said, "Call his name Jezreel; for yet a little while, and I will avenge the blood of Jezreel upon the house of Jehu" (Hos. 1:4).

11. Hosea's wife "bare a daughter. And God said unto him, Call her name Lo-ruhamah: for I will no more have mercy upon the house of Israel" (Hos. 1:6).

12. After Hosea's second son was born, God said, "Call his name Lo-ammi: for ye are not my people, and I will not be your God" (Hos. 1:9).

13. "Thou shalt call his name Jesus: for he shall save his people from their sins" (Matt. 1:21).

14. "The angel said unto him, Fear not, Zacharias: for thy prayer is heard; and thy wife Elisabeth shall bear thee a son, and thou shalt call his name John" (Luke 1:13).

15. Jesus said, "Thou art Simon the son of Jona: thou shalt be called Cephas" (John 1:42).

21

Odds and Ends

It would be difficult to compile one hundred and forty-one lists without gathering some lists that don't fit under any specific heading. Though not related to each other, the following lists should be of interest to you.

Did you realize that there are some extremely important bones mentioned in the Bible? There are also at least twenty-nine important stones recorded for us. Did you know that some battles were won supernaturally? Do you know how many times God's name is mentioned in the Bible? Here's one you probably haven't considered: did you know that the New Testament alone includes at least thirty-one descriptions of non-Christians?

143. Important Bones

1. "And of the rib, which the Lord God had taken from man, made he a woman" (Gen. 2:21,22).
2. "The bones of Joseph, which the children of Israel brought up out of Egypt, buried they in Shechem" (Josh. 24:32).
3. Samson "found a new jawbone of an ass, and put forth his hand, and took it, and slew a thousand men therewith" (Judges 15:15).
4. The men of Jabesh-gilead rescued the bones of Saul and his sons from Beth-shan and buried them under a tree at Jabesh (1 Sam. 31:11-13).
5. "And it came to pass, as they were burying a man, that behold, they spied a band of [Moabites]; and they cast the man into the sepulchre of Elisha: and when the man was let

166

down, and touched the bones of Elisha, he revived, and stood up on his feet" (2 Kings 13:20,21).

6. King Josiah desecrated the heathen altar at Bethel by burning human bones on it (2 Kings 23:16).
7. Ezekiel saw a valley of dry bones in a vision (Ezek. 37:1-14).
8. "But when the soldiers came to Jesus, and saw that he was dead already, they broke not his legs.... For these things were done, that the scripture should be fulfilled, A bone of him shall not be broken" (John 19:33,36).

Ezekiel's valley of dry bones

144. The Number of Times God, Jesus, and Satan Are Mentioned

1. The capitalized word *God* appears in the Bible 4,395 times.
2. The name *Jesus* appears in the Bible 979 times.
3. The name *Satan* appears in the Bible 56 times.

145. Thirty Important Stones

1. Jacob used a stone for a pillow at Bethel and dreamed about the Lord. In the morning, he took the stone and set it up as a pillar of remembrance before the Lord (Gen. 28:11-22).
2. "When Jacob saw Rachel . . . Jacob went near and rolled the stone from the well's mouth, and watered the flock of Laban" (Gen. 29:10,11).
3. Jacob and Laban made a heap of stones as a witness to their covenant not to bother one another (Gen. 31:44-52).
4. "God appeared unto Jacob again, when he came out of Padan-aram, and blessed him. . . . And Jacob set up a pillar in the place where he talked with him, even a pillar of stone" (Gen. 35:9,14).
5. The Lord told Moses, "Thou shalt smite the rock, and there shall come water out of it, that the people may drink" (Ex. 17:6).
6. While Amalek fought Israel, Moses sat on a stone while Aaron and Hur held his hands up to God (Ex. 17:8-12).
7. "The Lord said unto Moses, Come up to me into the mount, and be there: and I will give thee tables of stone, and a law, and commandments which I have written" (Ex. 24:12).
8. Aaron's ephod held two onyx stones engraved with the names of the children of Israel (Ex. 28:9-12).
9. "The Lord said unto Moses, Hew thee two tables of stone like unto the first: and I will write upon these tables the words that were in the first tables" (Ex. 34:1).
10. Joshua had twelve stones taken from the dry pathway across the Jordan to be set in a heap in Canaan as a memorial. He also had twelve stones piled up where the priests had stood in the river (Josh. 4:4-8).
11. As Joshua pursued the Amorites, "the Lord cast down great stones from heaven upon them" (Josh. 10:11).
12. The five Amorite kings fled from Joshua and hid in a cave.

Jacob dreams while resting his head on a stone

He rolled large stones over the entrance to hold them in (Josh. 10:16-18).

13. After the children of Israel had covenanted to serve the Lord, Joshua set up a stone as a witness to all that had been promised (Josh. 24:27).

14. "A certain woman cast a piece of a millstone upon Abimelech's head, and all to brake his skull" (Judges 9:53).

15. After the Israelites had defeated the Philistines, Samuel raised a stone pillar "and called the name of it Ebenezer, saying, Hitherto hath the Lord helped us" (1 Sam. 7:12).
16. "David put his hand in his bag, and took thence a stone, and slang it, and smote [Goliath] in his forehead" (1 Sam. 17:49).
17. "King [Solomon] commanded, and they brought great stones, costly stones, and hewed stones, to lay the foundation of the house" of the Lord (1 Kings 5:17).
18. After the priests of Baal had failed, Elijah took twelve stones, built an altar, and laid a bullock on top. The fire of the Lord fell and consumed even the stones" (1 Kings 18:31-38).
19. Nebuchadnezzar dreamed about a great image and then "a stone was cut out without hands, which smote the image upon his feet that were of iron and clay, and brake them to pieces" (Dan. 2:34,35).
20. Daniel was thrown into the lions' den, and it was sealed with a stone and the king's own signet (Dan. 6:17).
21. Jesus said, "Thou art Peter, and upon this rock I will build my church; and the gates of hell shall not prevail against it" (Matt. 16:18).
22. "Jesus saith unto them, Did you never read in the scriptures, The stone which the builders rejected, the same is become the head of the corner?" (Matt. 21:42).
23. After laying Jesus in the tomb, Joseph of Arimathaea "rolled a great stone to the door of the sepulchre" (Matt. 27:59,60).
24. Jesus prophesied about the temple, saying, "There shall not be left one stone upon another that shall not be thrown down" (Mark 13:1,2).
25. The devil tempted Jesus, saying, "If thou be the son of God, command this stone that it be made bread" (Luke 4:3).
26. Jesus told the Pharisees that if the people did not hail Him king, the stones would cry out (Luke 19:40).
27. Before He called Lazarus from the grave, Jesus ordered that the stone be removed from the entrance of the tomb (John 11:38-40).
28. The children of Israel "drank of that spiritual rock that followed them: and that Rock was Christ" (1 Cor. 10:4).
29. "The Spirit saith unto the churches; To him that overcometh will I give ... a white stone" (Rev. 2:17).
30. An angel took up a stone like a great millstone and threw it into the sea in John's vision (Rev. 18:21).

146. Lamps and Candles

1. Abraham set up a sacrifice to God to confirm the covenant, and God took a burning lamp through the midst of the sacrifice as a sign of His promise (Gen. 15:17).
2. The Lord commanded Moses to make a seven-branched candlestick to be placed within the tabernacle (Ex. 25:31-37).
3. Gideon's men "blew the trumpets, and brake the pitchers, and held the lamps in their left hands, . . . and they cried, The sword of the Lord, and of Gideon" (Judges 7:16-21).
4. David sang, "For thou art my lamp, O Lord: and the Lord will lighten my darkness" (2 Sam. 22:29).
5. "Thy word is a lamp unto my feet, and a light unto my path" (Ps. 119:105).
6. Jesus said, "Ye are the light of the world. A city that is set on a hill cannot be hid" (Matt. 5:14).
7. "Then shall the kingdom of heaven be likened unto ten virgins, which took their lamps, and went forth to meet the bridegroom" (Matt. 25:1).
8. "What woman having ten pieces of silver, if she lose one piece, doth not light a candle, and sweep the house, and seek diligently till she find it?" (Luke 15:8).
9. The Philippian jailor called for a light to see if his prisoners were still in the jail (Acts 16:29).
10. John saw Jesus walking among seven golden candlesticks in his vision on Patmos (Rev. 1:12).
11. John described the new Jerusalem, saying, "There shall be no night there; and they need no candle, neither light of the sun; for the Lord God giveth them light" (Rev. 22:5).

147. Ten Battles Won Supernaturally

1. The Lord destroyed the Egyptian army in the Red Sea (Ex. 14:13-31).
2. "And it came to pass, when Moses held up his hand, that Israel prevailed: and when he let down his hand, Amalek prevailed" (Ex. 17:11).
3. When Joshua fought the kings of the Amorites, the Lord caused the sun to stand still, and He threw large hailstones down from the sky to kill the fleeing Amorites (Josh. 10:6-13).

4. "The Philistines drew near to battle against Israel: but the Lord thundered with a great thunder on that day upon the Philistines, and discomfited them; and they were smitten before Israel" (1 Sam. 7:10).
5. Jonathan and his armor-bearer attacked the Philistines, and the Lord sent an earthquake that routed the enemy before them (1 Sam. 14:11-15).
6. "Israel won a battle against the Syrians when the Lord struck the Syrians blind at Elisha's word (2 Kings 6:18-23).
7. "The Lord had made the host of the Syrians to hear a noise of chariots, and a noise of horses, even the noise of a great host. . . . Wherefore they arose and fled in the twilight" (2 Kings 7:6-7).
8. The Lord saved Jerusalem from the Syrians when "the angel of the Lord went out, and smote in the camp of the Assyrians an hundred fourscore and five thousand" (2 Kings 19:35).
9. "As the men of Judah shouted, it came to pass, that God smote Jeroboam and all Israel before Abijah and Judah. And the children of Israel fled before Judah" (2 Chron. 13:15-16).
10. Jehoshaphat and Judah "began to sing and to praise, [and] the Lord set ambushments against the children of Ammon, Moab, and mount Seir, which were come against Judah; and they were smitten" (2 Chron. 20:22).

148. Thirty-one New Testament Descriptions of Sinful Mankind

1. Alienated from God (Eph. 4:18).
2. Blind (John 12:40; 2 Cor. 4:4; 1 John 2:11).
3. Carnally or fleshly minded (Rom. 8:6,13).
4. Corrupt (Matt. 7:17-18; 1 Tim. 6:5).
5. Darkened (Matt. 6:23; John 3:19; Rom. 1:21; Eph. 4:18; 1 John 1:6-7).
6. Dead in sin (John 5:24; Rom. 8:6; Col. 2:13; 1 Tim. 5:6; 1 John 3:14).
7. Deceived (Titus 3:3).
8. Defiled or filthy (Isa. 64:6; Titus 1:15; 2 Pet. 2:20; Rev. 22:11).
9. Destitute of truth (Rom. 1:18, 25; 1 Tim. 6:5).
10. Disobedient (Matt. 7:23; Eph. 2:3; Titus 3:3).

The angel destroys the Assyrian army

11. An enemy of God (James 4:4).
12. Evil (Matt. 6:22; 12:33-34; John 3:20).
13. Foolish (Matt. 7:26; Eph. 5:15; Titus 3:3).
14. Going astray (1 Pet. 2:25).
15. Hateful (Titus 3:3).
16. Hypocritical (Matt. 6:2,5,16; 23:13,28).
17. Impenitent (Rom. 2:5; Heb. 3:8).

18. Malicious and envious (Titus 3:3).
19. Pleasure or world-loving (2 Thess 2:12; 1 Tim. 5:6; 2 Tim. 3:4; Titus 3:3; 1 John 2:15).
20. Proud (Rom. 1:30; 1 Tim. 6:4; 2 Tim. 3:4; James 4:6; 1 Pet. 5:5).
21. Refusing belief (John 3:35; Titus 1:15).
22. Rejecting truth (2 Tim. 4:4).
23. Resisting God (Acts 7:51).
24. Guided by Satan (John 8:44; Eph. 2:3).
25. Lovers of self (2 Tim. 3:2).
26. Self-satisfied (Rev. 3:17).
27. A slave of sin (John 8:34; Rom. 6:16-17,20; Titus 3:3).
28. Subordinating God (Rom. 1:25).
29. Unconscious of bondage (John 8:33; Rom. 7:7).
30. Unrighteous (1 Cor. 6:9; Rev. 22:11).
31. Vain in their imaginations (Rom. 1:21).

149. Thirty Important Theological Terms Found in the Bible

1. *Adoption* (Gr. *huiothesia*)—Adoption is that act of God's grace by which He brings men into His family and makes them partakers of all the blessings He has provided for them. Adoption represents an entirely new relationship into which the believer is introduced via justification, and the privileges connected therewith—viz., an interest in God's love (John 17:23; Rom. 5:8); a spiritual nature (Rom. 8:15-21; Gal. 5:1; Heb. 2:15); present protection and consolation (John 14:18; 2 Cor. 1:4); and a future glorious inheritance (Rom. 8:17, Phil. 3:21).

2. *Atonement* (Gr. *katallage*)—The atonement of Christ refers to that work by which forgiveness of sins has been made possible. But in Scripture usage the word denotes the reconciliation itself and not just the means by which it was secured. When speaking of Christ's saving work, the "satisfaction" is to be preferred to the word "atonement." Christ's satisfaction is all He did in behalf of sinners to satisfy all the righteous demands of the broken law. Christ's sufferings were vicarious—i.e., were in our stead as our substitute. It must alway be kept in mind that the death of Christ is not the cause, but the *consequence* of God's love to guilty men (John 3:16; Rom. 3:24; Eph. 1:7; John 1:9).

3. *Birthright* (Gr. *prototokia*)—This word denotes certain privileges belonging to the firstborn son according to Jewish tradition. He became the priest of the family. Reuben was the firstborn of the patriarchs, and thus the priesthood of the tribes belonged to him. That honor, however, was transferred by God from Reuben to Levi (Num. 3:12, 13; 8:18). The firstborn also inherited the judicial authority of his father, whatever it might be (2 Chron. 21:3).

The Jews attached a sacred importance to the rank of "firstborn" and "firstbegotten" as applied to the Messiah (Rom. 8:29; Col. 1:18). As firstborn he has an inheritance superior to his brethren and is the only true priest.

4. *Baptism* (Gr. *baptisma*)—Since the Greek word *baptisma* has no English equivalent, it is transliterated as baptism. What the New Testament writers meant by *baptisma* is not agreed upon. The term is interpreted many different ways. For some it means the beginning of salvation. For others it means the entry into the church or a sign of the covenant. Some see it as an outword testimony to the new birth. It also has two metaphorical meanings: the baptism with the Holy Spirit (Matt. 3:11), and Jesus' passion (Matt. 20:22; Luke 12:50).

5. *Blasphemy* (Gr. *blasphemia*)—This word is used in the sense of speaking evil of God (Ps. 74:18; Isa. 52:5; Rom. 2:24; Rev. 13:1; and 16:9). It also signifies any kind of false or evil speech, or verbal abuse. The Jews accused Jesus of blasphemy when He claimed to be the Son of God (Matt. 26:25; Mark 2:7). Blasphemy against the Holy Spirit (Matt. 12:31; Luke 12:10) is regarded by some as a continued rejection of the gospel and hence unpardonable as long as the sinner remains in unbelief. Others regard the expression as designating the sin of attributing the works of the Holy Spirit to that of the devil.

6. *Covenant of Grace*—This is the eternal plan of redemption entered into by three persons of the Godhead, and carried out by them in its totality. In it the Father represented the Godhead in its indivisible sovereignty; and the Son, His people as their surety (Ps. 89:3; Isa. 42:6; John 17:4, 6, 9).

The conditions of the covenant were:

1. On the part of the Father (a) all needful preparation of the Son for the accomplishment of his plan (Isa. 42:1-7; Heb. 10:5); (b) support in the work (Luke 22:43); and (c) a glorious

reward in Christ's final exaltation (Phil. 2:6-11).

    2. On the part of the Son the conditions were (a) His becoming incarnate (Gal. 4:4, 5) and (b) as the second Adam His representing all His people, assuming their place and undertaking the guilt due them and suffering the penalty of it (Isa. 53:2; 2 Cor. 5:21; Gal. 3:13) in their stead.

7. *Death* (Gr. *thanatos*)—Death may be defined simply as the termination of life. It is, however, used in a variety of ways in the Scriptures. (1) The dust shall "return to the earth as it was" (Eccles. 12:7). (2) "Thou takest away their breath, they die" (Ps. 104:29). (3) The dissolution of "our earthly house of this tabernacle" (2 Cor. 5:1; 2 Pet. 1:13, 14). (4) "Falling asleep" (Ps. 76:5; Jer. 51:39; Acts 13:36; 1 Thess. 4:14). (5) The departure of the spirit from the body (Eccles. 12:7; 2 Tim. 4:6).

    The "second death" (Rev. 2:11) is the everlasting perdition of the wicked (Rev. 21:8), and "second" in respect to natural or temporal death.

8. *Election* (Gr. *eklektos*)—In Christian theology this term usually refers to the divine choice of persons for salvation. On the one side, the doctrinal view usually known as Calvinism holds to unconditional election, where this choice is sovereign and in no way depends on man. The Arminians, on the other side, see all election as being in Christ and conditioned upon the individual's exercising a freewill trust in Christ.

9. *Evangelist* (Gr. *evangelistes*)—In biblical usage, a publisher of glad tidings; a missionary preacher of the gospel (Eph. 4:11). This title applied to Philip (Acts 21:8), who appears to have gone from city to city preaching the Word of God (8:4, 40). The writers of the four gospels are known as the Evangelists.

10. *Familiar spirit*—Sorcerers or necromancers, who claimed to be able to communicate with the spirits of the dead, were said to have a "familiar spirit" (Lev. 19:13; 20:6; 2 Chron. 33:6; Isa. 8:19). Sorcerers were regarded as vessels containing the inspiring demon. The Hebrew word *'ob* was equivalent to the Greek word *pytho*, and this word was used to signify both the person and the spirit which possessed him (Acts 16:16). The word "familiar" is from the Latin *familiaris*, meaning a "household servant," expressing the idea that sorcerers had spirits as their servants, ready to obey their commands.

11. *Forgive* (Gr. *aphienai*)—Forgiveness is one of the necessary

aspects of justification. When God forgives, He absolves the sinner from the condemnation of the law on the basis of the work of Christ. All sins are freely forgiven (Acts 5:31; 13:38; 1 John 1:6-9). By this act of grace, the sinner is freed from both the guilt and the penalty of his sins. This gracious act of God is offered in the gospel to all people.

12. *Gehena* (Gr. *Geena*)—Gehena was a deep, narrow glen southwest of Jerusalem, where, in Old Testament times, the idolatrous Jews offered their children in sacrifice to Molech (2 Chron. 28:3; 33:6; Jer. 7:31). At the time of Christ this valley was the common receptacle for all the refuse of the city. Here the dead bodies of animals and of criminals were cast and consumed by a continuously burning fire. In time it became the image of the place of everlasting destruction. This is what our Lord referred to in Matt. 5:22, 29, 30; 10:28; 18:9; 23:15, 33; Luke 12:5. In these passages, and also in James 3:6, the word is uniformly rendered "hell," the Revised Version placing "Gehenna" in the margin.

13. *Grace* (Gr. *charis*)—This term is used by biblical writers with much variety of meaning. Basic usage is as follows: (1) Of form or person (Ps. 45:2; Prov. 1:9; 3:22). (2) Favor, kindness, friendship (Gen. 6:8; 18:3; 19:19; 2 Tim. 1:9). (3) God's forgiving mercy (Rom. 11:6; Eph. 2:5). (4) The gospel as distinguished from the law of Moses (John 1:17; Rom. 6:14; 1 Pet. 5:12). (5) Gifts freely given by God such as miracles, prophecy, tongues (Rom. 15:15; 1 Cor. 15:10; Eph. 3:8). (6) The glory hereafter to be revealed (1 Pet. 1:13).

14. *Holy of Holies*—This was the second or interior portion of the tabernacle. It was left in total darkness to be lighted by God's glory. No one was permitted to enter it except the high priest and that only once a year, on the day of atonement. It contained the ark of the covenant (Ex. 25:10-16) and was in the form of a perfect cube of 20 cubits. It signified the geographic dwelling place of God among His people Israel. Immediately after the death of Christ, the veil in the temple separating the Holy Place and the Holy of Holies was torn from top to bottom by God himself. This action signified that all barriers to God's holy presence had been removed forever (Matt. 27:51; Heb. 9:12).

15. *Immanuel*—The meaning of this word is, God with us. In the

Old Testament it occurs only in Isa. 7:14 and 8:8. Most Christian interpreters have regarded these words as a direct and specific prophecy of our Savior—an interpretation born out by the words of the evangelist Matthew (1:23).

16. *Justification* (Gr. *dikaioo*)—Justification is the judicial act of God, by which He pardons all the sins of those who trust in Christ, and treats the believers as righteous in the eye of the law—i.e., as conformed to all its demands. In addition to the pardon of sin, justification declares that all the claims of the law are relaxed in respect of the justified. It is the act of a judge, not of a sovereign. The law is not set aside, but is declared to be fulfilled in the strictest sense, and the justified ones are now legally free. The sole condition on which this righteousness is credited to the believer is faith in the Lord Jesus Christ. Faith, here, is called a condition, not because it possesses any merit, but because it is the only instrument by which the soul appropriates or apprehends Christ and His righteousness (Rom. 1:17; 3:25; 4:20; Gal. 2:16; Phil. 3:8-11).

17. *Joy* (Gr. *chara*)—According to the Scriptures, joy is an attribute of God (Duet. 28:63; 30:9 Jer. 32:41) and second in the list of fruits of the Spirit catalogued by Paul (Gal. 5:22, 23). Joy is referred to countless times in Scripture, and is often mistakenly made synonymous with happiness, although the two qualities are quite different. Happiness tends to come out of circumstances that are happy, while joy comes despite the difficult circumstances of life (e.g., Paul and Silas were joyful in prison, Acts 16:23-33).

18. *Lord's Supper*—This was the ceremony instituted by our Lord, also called "the Lord's table" (1 Cor. 10:21), "communion," "cup of blessing" (10:16), and "breaking of bread" (Acts 2:42). The account of its institution is given in Matt. 26:26-29; Mark 14:22-25; Luke 22:19, 20, but not in John's gospel.

It was designed (1) to commemorate the death of Christ: "Do this in remembrance of me"; (2) to signify, seal, and apply to believers all the benefits of the new covenant; (3) to be an outer demonstration of the Christian faith; (4) to indicate and promote the communion of believers with Christ.

The elements used to represent Christ's body and blood are bread and wine. Christ used unleavened bread because it was on the paschal table. Wine is to be used (Matt. 26:26-29). Believers partake of the elements and all that the elements stand for. This "feeding" on Christ, however, takes place not in the Lord's Supper alone, but whenever faith in Him is exercised.

19. *Lamb of God*—In the symbolic language of Scripture, Jesus was called the Lamb of God (John 1:29), emphasizing the redemptive work of Christ. More than twenty times in the book of Revelation the lamb is found as the symbol of Christ.

The Old Testament institutes the lamb as the sacrificial victim. Of special interest is the Passover lamb (Ex. 12:3-6). With the sacrifice of this lamb, deliverance from Egypt was secured. This deliverance symbolized God's redemption from sin as accomplished in Christ (Luke 9:31; 1 Cor. 5:7).

20. *Manna* (Heb. *manhu*)—Manna is the name given by the Israelites to the food miraculously supplied to them during their wilderness wanderings (Ex. 16:15-35). The name is commonly assumed as derived from an expression of surprise, "What is it?" (Heb. *man*). It is described as a "small round thing" like the "hoarfrost of the ground" and tasting like a "wafer made with honey." It was capable of being baked and boiled, ground in a mill, or beaten in a mortar (Ex 16:23; Num. 11:7). If any remained until the following morning, it would spoil. Since no manna fell on the Sabbath, a double portion was to be gathered the preceding day; this could be kept overnight to supply the wants of the Sabbath without spoiling. Directions for the gathering of it are fully given in Ex. 16:16-18, 33 and in Deut. 8:3, 16.

In the New Testament our Lord refers to the manna when He calls himself the "true bread from heaven" (John 6:31-35; 48:51). He is also the "hidden manna" (Rev. 2:17).

21. *Mercy Seat* (Heb. *kapporeth*; Gr. *hilasterion*)—The mercy seat constituted the upper covering or lid of the Ark of the Covenant. Constructed of acacia wood, it was overlaid with gold, or perhaps a plate of solid gold, 2½ cubits long and 1½ broad (Ex. 25:17; 30:6; 31:7). It is compared to the throne of grace (Heb. 9:5; Eph. 2:6). The Holy of Holies is called the "place of the mercy seat" (1 Chron. 28:11; Lev. 16:2).

Some have thought that the censer mentioned in Heb. 9:4 was the "mercy seat" at which the incense was burned by the high priest on the great day of atonement, and upon or toward which the blood of the goat was sprinkled (Lev. 16:11-16; cf. Ex. 25:22 and Num. 7:89).

22. *Messiah* (Heb. *mashiah*)—In all 39 places where this word

occurs in the Old Testament, it is rendered by the Septuagint as *christos*, which means anointed. The distinction between the anointings the prophets and priests received and which the Messiah himself received is that the Messiah is anointed "above his fellows" (Ps. 45:7). The Greek form "Messias" is used only twice in the New Testament (John 1:41; 4:25. In English versions of the Old Testament the word Messiah, as the rendering of the Hebrew, occurs only twice (Dan. 9:25, 26).

23. *Paradise*—Paradise is derived from an early Persian word (*pardes*), properly meaning a "pleasure-ground" or "park," or "king's garden." Scholars feel it was introduced into the Greek language at a very early date and eventually came to be used as a name for the world of happiness and rest hereafter (Luke 23:43; 2 Cor. 12:4; Rev. 2:7).

24. *Pentecost* (Gr. *pentecoste*)—The word Pentecost is found only in the New Testament (Acs 2:1; 20:16; 1 Cor. 16:8). This festival is first spoken of in Ex. 23:16 as the "feast of harvest" and again in Ex. 32:22 as the "feast of weeks." The purpose of the feast was to commemorate the completion of the grain harvest. The high point of this celebration was the offering of "two leavened loaves" made from the new grain which, with two lambs, were waved before the Lord as a thank offering.

The day of Pentecost is noted in the Christian Church as the day on which the Spirit descended upon those gathered in the upper room, and those who were converted under Peter's preaching.

25. *Repentance* (Gr. *metamelomai/metanoeo*)—The verb *metamelomai* is used of a change of mind, such as to produce regret or even remorse on account of sin, but not necessarily a change of heart. This word is used with reference to the repentance of Judas (Matt. 27:3).

Metanoeo is the stronger of the two words and signifies a change of mind *and* purpose. This verb and the cognate noun, *metanoia*, are used of true repentance—a change of mind and purpose of life to which remission of sin is promised.

Evangelical repentance consists of a true sense of one's guilt, an apprehension of the hope there is in Christ, a hatred for sin and the willingness to turn from it and forsake it (Job 42:5, 6; Ps. 119:128; 2 Cor. 7:10).

26. *Regeneration* (Gr. *palingenesia*)—The word regeneration,

found only in Matt. 19:28 and Titus 3:5, literally means a new birth. In Matt. 19:28 the word is equivalent to the "restitution of all things" (Acts 3:21). In Titus 3:5, it denotes that change of heart elsewhere spoken of as passing from death to life (1 John 3:14); becoming a new creature in Christ (2 Cor. 5:17); being born again (John 3:5); a renewal of mind (Rom. 12:2); resurrection from the dead (Eph. 2:6); and being quickened (2:1, 5). This change is ascribed to the Holy Spirit, for it originates with God and not man. The change consists of the implanting of a new principle or disposition in the soul; the impartation of spiritual life to those who are dead in trespasses and sins. The necessity of such a change is emphatically affirmed in Scripture (John 3:3; Rom. 7:18; 1 Cor. 2:14; Eph. 2:1; 4:21-24).

27. *Tribulation, Great Tribulation* (Gr. *thlipsis*)—Scriptural usage of the term denotes trouble or affliction of any kind (Deut. 4:30; Matt. 13:21; 2 Cor. 7:4). In Rom, 2:9, "tribulation and anguish" are the penal sufferings that shall overtake the wicked. In Matt. 24:21, 29, the word signifies the calamities that were to attend the destruction of the temple and city of Jerusalem.

The Great Tribulation, however, is a definite period of unprecedented divine wrath sent from God upon the earth for the dual purposes of judgment and purging (Dan. 12:1; Matt. 24:21). Three major theological opinions exist as to when this judgment period will begin. According to the premillennial view, it precedes the millennial reign of Christ. The postmillennial view places it at the end of the one thousand years, and the amillennial view places it just before the new heavens and new earth are brought in.

28. *Truth* (Gr. *aletheia*)—In ancient literature this term was employed to descibe that which was merely the opposite of a lie. Although this definition is found in the Scriptures (Prov. 12:17-19), the biblical term is of greater significance. That greater significance rests within the person of Christ himself: Jesus is the source of all truth (John 1:14; 14:6); His word is truth (John 5:30; 8:26); His judgments are true (John 8:6).

29. *Temptation* (Gr. *peirasmos*)—A sharp biblical distinction is drawn between the testings and trials of life and those temptations that are enticements to moral evil. Men are "tempted" or "put to the test" to try their faith and patience, but God himself is never the author of the temptation to evil.

These tempations come from the inordinate affections of the flesh and the wiles of the evil one himself; hence, Satan is called "the tempter." The Scriptures inform us that temptation is common to all (Ps. 66:10; Dan. 12:10; Luke 22:31; Heb. 11:17; James 1:12), but temptation itself is not sin. Rather, it is the yielding of the will to the temptation that brings guilt.

30. *Propitiation* (Gr. *hilasmos*)—Propitiation is that act of God by which it becomes consistent with His character and government to pardon and bless the sinner. This propitiation does not procure His love or make Him loving; it only renders it consistent for Him to extend pardon toward sinners. In Rom. 3:25 and Heb. 9:5 the Greek word *hilasterion* is used. This word came to denote reconciliation by blood. On the great day of atonement the high priest carried the blood of the sacrifice, which he offered for all the people, within the veil and sprinkled the mercy seat of the Ark; in so doing, he made propitiation for the people.

In 1 John 2:2 and 4:10, Christ is called the "propitiation for our sins." Here, however, a different Greek word is used (*hilasmos*). Christ is the propitiation because by His becoming our substitute and by His vicarious death, He has taken upon himself the guilt of our sins.

150. Eleven Scriptures Commonly Misinterpreted by the Jehovah's Witnesses and Mormons

1. *John 1:1:* "In the beginning was the Word, and the Word was with God, and the Word was God."

Correct meaning: The last sentence clause ascribes the nature of deity to the preincarnate Christ.

Watchtower rendering: "In the beginning was the Word, the Word was with God and the Word was *a god*" (NWT).

Watchtower interpretation: By inserting the word "a" into the last sentence clause, the Jehovah's Witnesses claim that Jesus was *a* god. He was the first and greatest creation of Jehovah God, a subordinate god of secondary rank, but in no way equal with the Father in either nature or eternality.

Christian refutation: No matter how the Watchtower follower attempts to escape, the fact is, he still winds up with two gods (viz., Jehovah, the "big God," and Jesus, the "lesser god"). Yet Jehovah himself has declared, "I am the first, and I am the last; and beside me there is no God" (Isa. 44:6). There is only one God, not two. Isa. 43:10 also refutes the idea of a lesser god being created apart from Jehovah himself, "Ye are my witnesses, saith the Lord, and my servant whom I have chosen: that ye may know and believe me, and understand that I am he: *before me there was no God formed, neither shall there be after me.*" There are no other gods apart from Jehovah.

2. *John 8:58:* "Jesus said unto them, Verily, verily, I say to you, Before Abraham was I am."

Correct meaning: In this passage the Lord Jesus takes the divine name into His mouth. This was the same name God himself used as He confronted Moses at the burning bush (Ex. 3:14).

Watchtower rendering: "Jesus said unto them, truly, truly I say unto you, before Abraham was, I have been" (NWT).

Watchtower interpretation: In order to take the divine name from Christ, the Watchtower retranslated the "I am" of the last sentence clause to, "I have been." In the 1950 edition of the New World Translation, a footnote at John 8:58 defends the accuracy of the "I have been" rendering, owing to the "perfect indefinite tense" of the Greek language.

Christian refutation: The Watchtower Bible and Tract Society invented the so-called perfect indefinite tense. No such tense exists in New Testament Greek as any simple perusal of a Greek lexicon will show. In John 8:58 Jesus declares himself to be the great I AM; and the Pharisees understood Him perfectly as shown in their vehement desire to stone Him.

3. *John 14:28:* ". . . the Father is greater than I."

Correct meaning: While on the earth, and in His role as the earthly Messiah, and while humbly submitting himself to the will of His Father, Jesus could say that the Father was indeed greater than He.

Watchtower rendering: ". . . the Father is greater than I am" (NWT).

Watchtower interpretation: This passage is quoted as "proof" that Jesus cannot be equal with His Father, for how can Christ be equal in nature if Jesus himself declared His Father to be greater?

Christian refutation: As a man, and while in His earthly redemptive role, Jesus sacrificially laid aside His rights to exercise the full prerogatives of Deity (Phil. 2:6-8). In the circumstances of the incarnation, Jesus voluntarily laid aside and limited the exercise of the natural attributes of the divine nature (2 Cor. 8:9). The Father's position was indeed greater while Christ was on the earth. But greater does *not* mean better. By way of illustration we could say that the President of the United States is "greater" than anyone by virtue of his office. But we would never say that the President is *better* than others, for such a comparison would make his moral nature superior to those with whom the comparison was being made. The Scriptures never make such a comparison between the Father and the Son.

4. *Colossians 1:15:* "And he [Jesus] is the image of the invisible God, the firstborn of all creation."

Correct meaning: In context, verse 15 simply states that Jesus is the Preeminent One over all creation.

Watchtower rendering: Same as above.

Watchtower interpretation: Since Christ is called the "firstborn," this can only mean that He was the first *created.* Hence, Jesus cannot be co-eternal with the Father.

Christian refutation: The word firstborn (Gr. *prototokos*) has two meanings in the Scriptures, not just one. The first meaning is that of a literal firstborn son or daughter as in Luke 2:7 where Jesus is referred to as Mary's firstborn son. Here, the greek term *prototokos* is used. But this term is also used as a title to denote ranking authority or kingly preeminence. This is seen in the life of Ephraim (Gen. 41:50-52). Even though Ephraim was not the firstborn of Joseph's sons (Jer. 31:9), he is nevertheless declared the firstborn. The explanation is found in Genesis 48 where Ephraim was given ranking preeminence over his brother Manasseh via the blessing of his grandfather Jacob. Thus, Ephraim, who was *not* the firstborn, was given the title of firstborn, not by birth, but by inheritance blessing! In the Septuagint, the Greek translation of the Old Testament, the same Greek term that Paul uses to designate Christ as the firstborn (*prototokos*) is used of Ephraim in Jer. 31:9. Also, in Ps. 89:20-27, David is called the "firstborn." David was not Jessie's firstborn son, he received the title because of the kingly preeminence given to him within the context of this Psalm. Again, the Greek term *prototokos* is used, refuting the claim that *prototokos* only means "first created."

In the context of Colossians 1, Christ is declared to be the Preeminent One over all creation. Like Ephraim who was not the firstborn but was called the firstborn, and like David who received the title firstborn, Jesus, owing to His authority over all things, is rightly called the firstborn, *not* by creation, but via His ranking authority and kingly preeminence over all.

5. *Colossians 1:16, 17:* "For by him were all things created that are in heaven and that are on earth, visible and invisible, whether they be thrones or dominions or principalities or powers—all things were created by him and for him. And he is before all things, and by him all things consist."

Correct meaning: Jesus existed prior to all creation and is, in fact, the creator of all things.

Watchtower rendering: "Because by means of him all [other] things were created in the heavens and upon the earth . . . all [other] things have been created through him and for him. Also, he is before all [other] things and by means of him all [other] things were made to exist" (NWT). [Brackets are from the NWT.]

Watchtower interpretation: The word "other" makes Christ a creature, one of the things that is spoken of as having been created.

Christian refutation: The Watchtower Society inserted the word "other" into the text even though no existing Greek manuscript contains it. This is a deliberate attempt to reduce the Son of God from creator to creature. No reputable translator dares tamper with a doctrinal text in such fashion. Since this passage clearly teaches the existence of Christ before the creation of *all things*, and since He is the creator of these things, He himself cannot possibly be a part of the creation He is said to have created. He could not create himself! There are only two categories: 1) God, 2) creation. If Jesus Christ is not a part of the creation, He can only be Almighty God.

6. *Revelation 3:14:* "And unto the angel of the church of the Laodiceans write: These things saith the Amen, the faithful and true witness, the beginning of the creation of God."

Correct meaning: Jesus Christ is the source, or origin, of all God's creation.

Watchtower rendering: "And to the angel of the congregation in Laodicea write: these are the things that the Amen says, the faithful and true witness, the beginning of the creation by God" (NWT).

Watchtower interpretation: Jesus must be a creature, for this passage declares Him to have had a beginning.

Christian refutation: The English word "beginning" is translated from the Greek word *arche*, which could be correctly rendered as origin. The Watchtower itself is forced to admit this, for in the 1950 edition of their own New World Translation, they rendered *arche* as "originally" in their translation of John 1:1. Thus, by their own admission, *arche* can be translated as origin. For this reason, Christ is the *arche*—the origin, source, or the beginning of creation—for it is through Christ that all the creation came. He is the one who brought creation forth. Numerous other translations agree with this rendering of *arche* as source or origin, and in no sense whatsoever does this passage set forth the doctrine of a created Christ.

7. *John 10:34:* "Jesus answered them and said, Is it not written in your law, I said ye are gods?"

Mormon interpretation: This passage proves the existence of more than one God because of the plural use of the word "gods" in the last sentence clause.

Christian refutation: The word "gods" is derived from the Hebrew word *elohim* and has a variety of Old Testament usages. It can mean God, gods, rulers, judges, or magistrates. *Context must determine usage.* Upon a closer examination of John 10, we see that Jesus was actually quoting Ps. 82:6 to the Pharisees. Even a quick reading of Psalm 82 would reveal which of the meanings of *elohim* is intended and it will also become abundantly clear as to why Jesus chose to quote this particular Psalm to His opponents. For in this Psalm, God applies the word *elohim* to the judges of ancient Israel and rebukes them, for they were guilty of the same thing that Jesus charged the Pharisees with—perverting the judgment. Hardly a desirable attribute for one who aspires to godhood! In the Psalm Jesus quoted from, the meaning of the word "gods" is that of judges or rulers, and in no way does this passage teach a plurality of gods.

8. *1 Corinthians 8:5:* "For though there be that are called gods, whether in heaven or in earth (as there be gods many and lords many)."

Mormon interpretation: The words "gods many and lords many" prove the doctrine of the plurality of Gods.

Christian refutation: The "gods many and lords many" of verse 5 are identified in context as the gods and goddesses of the Greek and Roman world (vv. 1, 4, 10). The Mormon interpretation ignores both immediate and historic context, thus reading into the text that which the author did not intend. (Paul was writing to Christians who had been converted *out* of a pagan society that believed in the existence of many gods—"gods many and lords many.") But since there is but *one* God who is God "by nature" (Gal. 4:8; Acts 17:24, 25, and since that one God has declared that there were no gods formed before Him and none shall be formed after Him (Isa. 43:10), the Mormon interpretation of 1 Cor. 8:5 is shown to be spurious.

9. *Hebrews 5:4:* "And no man taketh this honor unto himself, but he that is called of God, as was Aaron."

Mormon interpretation: Mormonism claims this verse teaches that a person can minister the ordinances of the Christian Church only if that person himself has been ordained by one before him with the proper "authority." Since the Mormon church claims that it is the only church *with* that authority, Heb. 5:4 is used to show Christians in general, and Christian workers in particular, that they have no right or authority to declare their faith or administer the ordinances of baptism or the Lord's Supper. Hence, Christians have taken this honor of administering the ordinances unto themselves without the proper authority.

Christian refutation: The honor spoken of here is *not* the authority to exercise the Christian ordinances of baptism or the Lord's Supper. Both immediate context and comparative textual analysis identify the honor being spoken of here as that of the high priestly office of Aaron.

vs. 1 "every high priest . . . offers gifts and sacrifices for sins" (the very function of the Aaronic high priest)

vs. 2 (this high priest) is compassed with infirmity (as were the high priests of the Aaronic order)

vs. 3 so also for himself to offer for his sins (Lev. 16:6; Heb. 7:27; 9:7 tells us this is exactly what the high priests of the Aaronic order had to do)

vs. 4 No man taketh this honor unto himself (which was also true of the priesthood of Aaron as severe penalties were meted out to those who tried to become priests and who were not of the proper tribe and house—truly, no man could take this honor unto himself)

Heb. 5:4 is simply a New Testament statement of the situation as it existed in Old Testament times regarding the divinely imposed restrictions as to who could and could not join themselves to the priesthood. It states that no one under the old economy could take the office of the priesthood without proper authority. But to use this verse in an attempt to prohibit Christians from receiving or administering the Christian ordinances is to ignore both immediate context and the entire message of the book of Hebrews itself! The book of Hebrews plainly declares that the Aaronic priesthood has been superseded by the infinitely superior ministry of the Lord Jesus Christ and that the priesthood of Aaron was after Christ's death on the cross. The way into the presence of God has been forever opened by the death of Christ. Authority is received when a person becomes a Christian (John 1:12). Since all authority in heaven and earth belongs to Jesus (Matt. 28:18) and since Christ has shared His very throne rights with those who know and love Him (Eph. 2:6), the Christian's authority lies not in a church or priesthood but in the very person of Jesus himself.

10. *Colossians 1:15:* (See under item #5.)

Mormon interpretation: It is claimed that this passage proves that Christ was the firstborn spirit-child between heavenly father and heavenly mother. This interpretation reduces Christ to a creature.

Christian refutation: (See Item #5 for interpretation of the word "firstborn.") The Jehovah's Witnesses reduce Christ to a creature via an act of creation by God the Father; the Mormons reduce Christ to a creature via a procreative act between God the father and one of His wives! Apart from the fact that the methods differ in the respective systems, the effect is the same—a created Christ. Both groups are undoubtedly ignorant that they are guilty of the other's heresy, though each claims to be the only true way to salvation!

11. *Ezekiel 37:15-17:* "The word of the Lord came again unto me, saying, Moreover, thou son of man, take thee one stick, and write upon it, For Judah, and for the children of Israel his companions: then take another stick, and write upon it, For

Joseph, the stick of Ephraim, and for all the house of Israel and his companions: and join them one to another into one stick; and they shall become one in thine hand."

Mormon interpretation: The two sticks prophetically symbolize two books—the Bible and the Book of Mormon. The joining together of the two sticks is meant to show the joining of the Bible and the Book of Mormon as necessary complements one to another. Thus the Bible itself bears witness to and prophesies the coming forth of the Book of Mormon.

Christian refutation: Using such farfetched principles of interpretation, the Bible could be used to say anything the reader wants it to. The Mormon claim that the two sticks prophetically symbolize the coming forth of two books carries about as much validity as claiming that the tower of Babel prophetically symbolizes the coming forth of the Brooklyn Bridge. The absurdity of the latter is no greater than the absurdity of the former. It is presumptuous to ignore God's explanation of the passage and seek to invent one's own. This explanation of the sticks is found within the passage itself (vv. 18-22). The sticks are indeed symbolic, but they symbolize two nations under one king, *not* two books in the hand of one church.

Abbreviations Used in this Book

1 Chron.	1 Chronicles	Mal.	Malachi
2 Chron.	2 Chronicles	Matt.	Matthew
Col.	Colossians	Mic.	Micah
1 Cor.	1 Corinthians	Neh.	Nehemiah
2 Cor.	2 Corinthians	Num.	Numbers
Dan.	Daniel	1 Pet.	1 Peter
Deut.	Deuteronomy	2 Pet.	2 Peter
Eccles.	Ecclesiastes	Phil.	Philippians
Eph.	Ephesians	Prov.	Proverbs
Ex.	Exodus	Ps.	Psalms
Ezek.	Ezekiel	Rev.	Revelation
Gal.	Galatians	Rom.	Romans
Gen.	Genesis	1 Sam.	1 Samuel
Hab.	Habakkuk	2 Sam.	2 Samuel
Hag.	Haggai	Song of Sol.	Song of Solomon
Heb.	Hebrews	1 Thess.	1 Thessalonians
Hos.	Hosea	2 Thess.	2 Thessalonians
Isa.	Isaiah	1 Tim.	1 Timothy
Jer.	Jeremiah	2 Tim.	2 Timothy
Josh.	Joshua	Zech.	Zechariah
Lam.	Lamentations	Zeph.	Zephaniah
Lev.	Leviticus		

Bibliography

Abbreviated Bible, The—with the Apocrypha
    by James Leslie McCary and Mark McElhaney
    Published by Van Nostrand Reinhold Co.
    Copyright 1971
Aids to Understanding the Holy Bible—
Appendix to *Family Bible*
    General Editor John Rea
    Published by the World Publishing Co.
    Copyright 1968
All the Men of the Bible
    by Herbert Lockyer
    Published by Zondervan Publishing House
    Copyright 1958, 26th printing, January 1979
Bible Dictionary—Concordance to Holy Bible,
Appendix to King James Version
    Published by A. J. Holman Co.
    Copyright 1942
Halley's Bible Handbook
    by Henry H. Halley
    Published by Zondervan Publishing House
    Copyright 1965, 24th edition
Interlinear Greek-English New Testament
    by Rev. Alfred Marshall D. Litt
    Published by Zondervan Publishing House
    Copyright 1958, 2nd edition, June 1969 reprint
Meredith's Book of Bible Lists
    by J. L. Meredith
    Published by Bethany House Publishers
    Copyright 1980
Strong's Exhaustive Concordance of the Bible
    by James Strong
    Published by Abingdon Press
    Copyright 1890, 25th printing, 1963
Unger's Bible Dictionary
    by Merrill F. Unger
    Published by Moody Press
    Copyright 1957, 1961, 1966, 3rd edition, 33rd printing, 1981

Universal Bible Dictionary, The
Edited by A. R. Buckland & Assisted by A. Luky Williams
Published by Fleming H. Revell Co.
No Copyright, 1951 edition
Wycliffe Bible Commentary, The
Edited by Charles F. Pfeiffer (O.T.) & Everett F. Harrison
(N.T.)
Published by Moody Press
Copyright 1962, 7th printing, 1972